*Bible Studies on*
# MARK

▶ ● ◀

## WILLIAM BOEKESTEIN

Reformed
Fellowship Inc.
www.reformedfellowship.net

Scripture taken from the New King James Version®.
Copyright © 1982 by Thomas Nelson, Inc. Used by permission.
All rights reserved.

For information:
*Reformed Fellowship, Inc.*
*(877) 532–8510*
*president@reformedfellowship*

Book design by Jeff Steenholdt

ISBN 978-1-935369-11-0

*To Jacqueline Sue Boekestein*
*for modeling Jesus' sacrificial service*
*in our home*

# Contents

# INTRODUCTION TO MARK'S GOSPEL

————————————►•◄————————————

## Mark 1:1

A number of years ago I was about to preach for the first time in a certain church. As I began to arrange my papers and books I noticed a sign on the top of the pulpit. It was a quotation from John 12:21 in which it is recorded that certain Greeks approached Philip and said to him, "Sir, we wish to see Jesus." I have since learned that many churches have placed these words on their pulpit as a reminder to the minister that one non-negotiable purpose of preaching is to show the glories of Christ to the congregation. I remember getting a little nervous as I thought about that sign, wondering if Christ was clearly set forth in my sermon. I'll never forget this event.

It is, of course, possible to lose sight of Christ in one's theology. But to do so is to forfeit the foundation of our faith. We become like Peter, who knew his theology but took his eyes off Jesus and began to sink in the sea. It is critically important for us to keep our eyes fixed on Jesus. One of the best ways to do so is to spend some time in the Gospels.

This first study introduces Mark's Gospel using his own preface: "the gospel of Jesus Christ." Mark tells us in his first verse that he has not written an epistle or a book of poetry but a Gospel. In so saying, Mark gives us a clue to help us understand his contribution to Holy Scripture.

## Introducing the Gospels

What is a Gospel, and why is this question critical in our study of this second book of the New Testament?

### The Gospels Are Narratives

"Broadly speaking, biblical truth comes in two basic literary forms, narrative and discourse. Narratives are stories" of historical events.[1] Gospels are distinct from poetry, or epistles, or prophecy, in that their teachings are couched in story.

The fact that the Gospels are narratives suggests several implications for how we study them. First, we need to keep the story form as much as possible. To take a tiny portion of a story and expound it at great length is to risk destroying the power of the story.[2]

Second, it is usually best to study one Gospel at a time. In other words, there is a place for judicious comparison with parallel Gospel accounts, but we should remember that "it is precisely their distinctives that are the reason for having four gospels in the first place."[3] So, for example, this study will not consider Jesus' birth narrative because Mark says nothing about it.

Third, we need to try to enter into the story as much as possible. A good story draws us in. And Mark, more than the other Gospel writers, includes the kind of details that help us imagine that we are in the story. Mark presents his message not as a dry lawyer's brief but as a fast-paced historical account of the ministry of the Savior of the world.

### The Gospels Are Prophetic Fulfillment

The Gospels are direct historical fulfillment of the Old Testament. Mark's second verse draws forward the testimony of the prophets: "As it is written in the prophets . . ." The Gospels essentially answer the question, "What has become of the message of the prophets?" Remember that the Old Testament had been completed around four hundred years before the first Gospels were written. During the intervening time there had been little to no prophetic movement. People were waiting and wondering, "Where is this promised Seed?" For this reason, Matthew begins with a genealogy. In his defense to Agrippa, Paul said that the only charge against him was that he had been saying "no other things than those which the prophets and Moses said would come—that the Christ would suffer, that He would be the first to rise from the dead and would proclaim light to the Jewish people and to the Gentiles" (Acts 26:22–23). Mark would have agreed with Paul.

*Gospels Are Good News*

Unlike other narratives, biblical narratives have a very specific purpose, namely, to describe the redemptive acts of God. "Gospel" comes from the Old English "godspell," or "good news." Gospels are theological biographies which announce the greatest story ever told (cf. Luke 1:1–4; Acts 1:1–3): Christ has come in the flesh to "deliver a ruined world, and to restore men from death to life."[4] As we study this Gospel we need to keep asking the question, "How does Jesus' life teach us good news?"

## Profiting from the Gospels

You probably wouldn't be reading this study if you didn't believe that it will be profitable to your spiritual life. One of simplest plans to profit from Mark's Gospel is to expect to see Jesus in His role as mediator. Christ came to fulfill the badly-deteriorated Old Testament offices of prophet, priest, and king (Jer. 8:1–3). As prophet He teaches us God's will; as king He rules over history and judges the thoughts, words, and deeds of men; and as priest He lays down His life to save his brethren. As we see Jesus in His threefold splendor, we respond as His loyal subjects.

*We Witness God's Redemptive Work in Christ*
When studying the Gospels we must ask, "Where is God in this story?" The Gospels help to give us a theological world and life view. The Gospels are different from modern histories in that their authors write from a transcendent viewpoint; they write from the perspective of God. They help explain the supernatural purposes lying behind the natural events.[5] This is how we need to see life. In order to be shaped by the theological history of the gospel we must not read the Gospels simply as moral lessons. The events in the Gospels are significant because they actually happened.

Biblical history is essentially the history of Christ. This is blatant in the Gospels. Other characters come in and out of the story, but the story never ceases to be about Jesus (even if none of them say everything about Christ).[6]

*We Observe the Life That God Blesses or Judges[7]*
When we read the Gospels we catch a glimpse of God interacting with men; in some cases blessing, in some cases cursing. We learn from these interactions what type of life God honors and which He rejects. We learn about this life in the Epistles through doctrine; in the Gospels through illustration.[8] Someone has said, "History is moral philosophy teaching by example."

We see the characters in narrative as mirrors. Sometimes we see an image that resembles us (for better or for worse). Sometimes we see an image that doesn't resemble us (again, for better or for worse). For example, we see Judas filled with remorse for his sins but not exhibiting true repentance (Matt. 27:3). We observe Pilate give in to crowd's pressure and refuse to do what he knew was right. We watch Peter confess Christ and then falter (Mark 15:1–15). The characters in the Gospels are literally living before the face of God in Christ. This fact cracks open a special window into our own lives as we seek to live before the face of God.

We must learn to ask, "Where am I in this story?"

*We Submit to the Great Teacher*

The epistle to the Hebrews begins by saying that God previously spoke by the prophets but "has in these last days spoken to us by His son, whom he has appointed heir of all things" (Heb. 1:1). God speaks to us through His Son. When Jesus was transfigured on the mountain God's voice boomed from heaven saying, "This is my beloved Son, hear Him!" (Mark 9:7). Jesus speaks through the entire Bible. But God insists that there is something unique about the prophetic earthly ministry of Christ recorded in the Gospels. In the words of Christ, the will of God takes on flesh and blood and communicates to us in a powerful way. If we did not have the Gospels we might miss God's tender invitations, His angry warnings, His solemn commands.

## Introducing Mark's Gospel

The more we know about this book the better we will be able to enter into it.

*The Author*[9]

Although we will talk about a human author of this book, the preeminent author is God the Holy Spirit. The Bible teaches that God moved holy men to record His very words (2 Peter 1:21). The book which we are undertaking to study is, properly speaking, God's Gospel, not Mark's.[10]

As the human author of the second Gospel, John Mark was not an apostle but a close associate of the apostle Peter, who calls him his son (1 Peter 5:13). He likely grew up right in the center of the exciting start of Christianity (Mark 14:51–52) because his mother, Mary, occupied a position of prominence and influence among the early Christians (Acts 12:12). He was present for part of the first missionary journey of Paul and Barnabas, who was his cousin (Acts 12:25; 13:13). Mark evidently proved himself faithful thereafter, for when

Paul was imprisoned in Rome he commended Mark to the Colossians (Col. 4:10). In fact, shortly before Paul died he requested Mark's presence (2 Tim. 4:11). By this time, Mark had probably written his Gospel.

When Mark first met Jesus he was likely a young man who had apparently grown up in a pious home. Those of us who have likewise grown up in Christian homes should take note: the life of Mark was anything but boring. Nor was it unproductive. He seems to have failed greatly on Paul's first journey. Yet he did not sulk in defeat but rather continued to labor for the Lord.

### Prominent Themes in Mark

As we begin our study it will be helpful to catch a glimpse of some of the themes we should expect to encounter along the way.

First, Mark focuses more on the works than the words of Christ (in comparison with the other Gospels).[11] Understanding this is helpful in two ways. First, it teaches us that we are to be not only talkers but also doers. The Gospel of Mark is a grand illustration of James's point that faith is made perfect by works (James 2:22). Second, it reminds us that Christ was a doer. We are not saved because Christ talked about the kingdom of God (as important as this is) but because He ushered in the kingdom of God by His deeds. He fought against Satan. He performed miracles. He faithfully walked this earth to fulfill the law's demands for us. As one commentator has said, Mark presents the ministry of Christ "as one of strenuous activity. Task follows task, with almost breathless rapidity."[12] It is not insignificant that Mark frequently prefaces Christ's action with the word *immediately.*[13] It is true that in His doing He sets a pattern for us, but He also comforts us with the promise that "it is done." Christ is the ultimate doer. He labored for us so that we could rest in Him. At the same time, Mark records ten occasions on which Jesus withdrew from the crowds to be alone with His disciples or with God.[14]

Second, Mark emphasizes Christ's passion. Mark devotes a greater proportion of his Gospel to the events surrounding Christ's death than Matthew, Luke, or John. He uses ten chapters to describe the first thirty-three years of Jesus' life, and five chapters to portray the week of His death. This dual emphasis is a beautiful picture of our redemption which is accomplished by both the active and passive obedience of Christ. We might say that Mark divides his Gospel into two scenes, although with significant thematic overlap. In the first scene Christ identifies with sinners. He demonstrates His power over evil through His miracles. He declares His power to forgive sins. He fulfills the will of God. This scene focuses on His active obedience. In the second scene He gives His life as a ransom. He is forsaken by both friends and Father. His blood falls to the sin-cursed ground. He paid the price for our disobedience. In His death, Christ's passive obedience shines like the stars on a dark night.

Third, Mark stresses the suffering nature of discipleship (8:34; 10:21). Throughout the Gospel, Mark makes it clear that to follow Jesus necessarily means to tread the path He trod. Mark's Gospel stresses that suffering always precedes glory; it did for Christ and it will for the Christian. We need to grasp this especially in light of the impact the health and wealth gospel has made on the church.

Fourth, Mark prioritizes Jesus' preaching of the kingdom; he uses the word *kingdom* at least twenty-one times. Louis Berkhof succinctly defines the kingdom as "the rule of God established and acknowledged in the hearts of sinners."[15] This definition of the kingdom helps us avoid two dangerous errors. First, we deny that the kingdom of God can be brought to bear by "human endeavors, such as education, [laws] or social reforms."[16] When Christ and the disciples preached the kingdom, they called men to repent and believe in Christ (1:15). Unless one's heart is changed, one cannot be an agent of change in the world. Second, we avoid the fallacy that suggests that true religion is strictly a private matter impotent to engage the world. When God changes our hearts, we become citizens of His kingdom who are obliged to use kingdom principles to make war against the gates of hell (Matt. 16:18).

The great irony is that Christ doesn't establish this kingdom through typical means of force but through suffering service. Charles Erdman has suggested that the key verse of Mark's Gospel is Mark 10:45, "The Son of man did not come to be served, but to serve, and to give His life a ransom for many." This is what we will see in the Gospel of Mark: The King of kings establishing a kingdom through service and sacrifice.

## Questions

1. What is a Gospel?
2. How is a Gospel both similar to and different from a biography?
3. Who is the author of the second Gospel? Explain.
4. What are some themes that are evident in the book of Mark?
5. Why might Mark's Gospel slow down near the end of Jesus' earthly ministry?
6. How is Jesus' constant activity in Mark a comfort for believers?
7. What are three questions that can help us profit from our study of the Gospels?
8. What are some practical implications of grasping Mark's theme of "victory through suffering"?
9. Reflect on the definition of "kingdom" offered in this study.

1. Dan Doriani, *Getting the Message: A Plan for Interpreting and Applying the Bible* (Phillipsburg, NJ: P&R, 1996), 61.

2. In preaching through a Gospel periscope it is best to follow the story line of the text. This seems to suggest that there should be manifest progress in a narrative sermon and sermon series. See Sidney Greidanus, *The Modern Preacher and the Ancient Text* (Grand Rapids: Eerdmans, 1988), 307.

3. Compare John Broadus, *Preparation and Delivery of Sermons* (New York: Hodder and Stoughton, 1898), 330, and Greidanus, *Modern Preacher and the Ancient Text,* 297.

4. From John Calvin's definition of Gospel in *Harmony of the Gospels,* vol. 1 (Grand Rapids: Baker Book House, 1989), xxxvi.

5. See Dan McCartney and Charles Clayton, *Let the Reader Understand: A Guide to Interpreting and Applying the Bible* (Phillipsburg, NJ: P&R, 2002), 224.

6. Compare John 21:30–31; 21:25, and William Klein, Craig Blomberg, and Robert Hubbard, *Introduction to Biblical Interpretation* (Nashville: Thomas Nelson, 2004), 400.

7. See Doriani, *Getting the Message,* 73–75.

8. Gordon Fee and Douglas Stuart, *How to Read the Bible for All It's Worth: A Guide to Understanding the Bible* (Grand Rapids: Zondervan, 1993), 83.

9. This section borrows from the clearly written introduction to Mark's Gospel found in Charles Erdman, *The Gospel of Mark* (Philadelphia: Westminster Press, 1945), 7–14.

10. Nonetheless, Jesus was comfortable with referring to the human author of Bible books (e.g., Luke 24:27).

11. Notably, Mark records very few of Jesus' parables (four) but a host of miracles (nineteen).

12. Erdman, *Gospel of Mark,* 11.

13. This word in the Greek is found forty-two times in Mark, which is more times than it is used in all the other books in the New Testament combined.

14. Erdman, *Gospel of Mark,* 12.

15. Louis Berkhof, *Systematic Theology* (Grand Rapids: Eerdmans, 1976), 408.

16. Berkhof, *Systematic Theology,* 408.

# PREPARATION FOR MINISTRY

**Mark 1:1–13**

Someone has said, "Preparation is half the battle." How often do plans fail for lack of preparedness? How often are we like the young man I once observed speaking with the manager of a gas station about getting a job? He was wearing his pajamas. His hair was a mess. He looked like he had just rolled out of bed. He was obviously not prepared for this interview and probably didn't get the job.

At the beginning of his Gospel, Mark teaches us the importance of preparation. His Gospel is a record of the most important plan ever enacted, the ministry of Jesus Christ. As we consider Jesus' preparation for his ministry, our faith in His finished work can be greatly strengthened.

Mark 1:2–13 distills three stages of Christ's incarnational ministry. In the first stage the people are being prepared by John the Baptist. In the second two stages the focus shifts to Christ's preparation. At the end of this brief account we rightly have high hopes for the ministry that is to follow.

## Christ's Herald (1:2–8)

Christ came to preach the good news of the kingdom of God, as the King of that kingdom. But every king has a herald, someone who goes before the king and announces his coming. Christ's herald was John.

Who was John the Baptist? If you would have asked *him*

that question he would have said, "I'm a nobody." He didn't want people to know who he was because he came to point people to Christ (John 3:30). In honor of John's request not to focus on himself we'll be brief. John was born under miraculous circumstances to Zacharias and Elizabeth. He lived in obscurity for most of his life. One day he came out of the wilderness, preached Christ with all his might for a short time, and was beheaded by Herod (Matt. 14:3, 10). He was a man who gave his life to Christ. Rather than focus on who John was we focus on three ways in which he served as a herald.

*John Came Fulfilling Prophesy*

John testified to Christ by being the one the Old Testament said would come to prepare His way. Appropriately, Mark uses the Old Testament to introduce Jesus' harbinger (vv. 2, 3). Mark first quotes from Malachi 3:1. In its broader context Malachi 3 foretells that the Messiah would come to judge the temple. Before this judgment God would send His messenger to prepare the way. By quoting from the last of the Old Testament prophets Mark skillfully links John the Baptist to the long line of messengers whom God sent to His people (Heb. 1:1).

Mark then quotes from Isaiah 40:3. Isaiah 40 begins Isaiah's message of comfort. Before the Messiah would come to deliver His people they would hear "the voice of one crying in the wilderness: 'Prepare the way of the Lord; make His paths straight.'" Isaiah said that a messenger would cry out in the wilderness; Mark 1:4 says that John came baptizing and crying out in the wilderness.

Mark introduces John the Baptist with these two passages to show the dual purpose of Christ's coming: to judge the illegitimate sons of the kingdom and to deliver His true sons from bondage to sin. John serves as Christ's herald by fulfilling the Old Testament prophecies which predicted that Christ would have a forerunner.

John's role as forerunner is also shown by his style (1:6). Mark's reference to John's camel-hair clothing and leather belt seem strange until we understand their purpose. John is here compared with Elijah, who was a hairy man who wore a leather belt (2 Kings 1:8). The last two verses of the Old Testament (Mal. 4:5–6) say that Elijah would return before Messiah. Mark here suggests what Christ would blatantly state: Elijah has come (cf. Mark 9:13)!

## John Came Preaching a Baptism of Repentance

John's message of repentance is a perfect hinge between the law-dominated Old Testament and the gospel-saturated New Testament.[1]

So important was John's message that it is highlighted by a visible symbol of baptism. In general, baptism is a sign of covenant membership and of identification with the people of God. But here baptism focuses on personal sinfulness. John heralds Christ's coming through baptism by emphasizing the reason for His coming: to remit sins. Baptism symbolizes our need for cleansing. For believers it is a seal of the forgiveness of sins and a call to new obedience. If you have been baptized, then you are identified as someone who has a sin problem. You have also been identified as one who can look confidently to Christ for forgiveness of sins.

## John Came Magnifying Christ

John magnifies Christ through two sayings (vv. 6–8). First, John speaks of his own unworthiness compared with Christ. "Christ is so great that I am not worthy to touch His shoes!" Not His feet, but His shoes! As evidence of his union with Christ, John thought great things of Christ and spoke great things of him. John's faith was anything but private!

Second, John says that although he baptized with water, Christ will baptize with the Spirit (v. 8). John makes the point that there is a difference between him as the outward administrator of baptism and Christ as the "author of spiritual baptism."[2] Mark insists, early in his record, that the Messiah is no mere man. After all, who can command the Spirit of God but God Himself?

## Christ's Baptism (1:9–11)

John's baptism prefaces the baptism of Christ, which provides an opportunity to reflect on the name "Christ."

### The Name "Christ"

In the baptism of Jesus His title of Messiah (from the Hebrew for "anointed one"; the Greek form is "Christ"), though not used, is graphically illustrated. To understand this important concept we need to look to the Old Testament. The kings of Israel were anointed with oil and thereby singled out for the office to which they had been called. Likewise, when King Jesus is introduced by His herald, He too is anointed, not with oil but with the Holy Spirit in His baptism. Christ was anointed to be a mediator, or one who bring resolution to two parties in conflict. Christ's baptism is His ordination service.[3]

The mediatorial nature of Christ's ministry is clearly seen from the way Christ identifies with both man and God in His baptism.

### Christ's Identification with Man

Mark tells us that Jesus came from Nazareth of Galilee for His baptism. This seemingly small detail is quite important. When the disciple Nathanael heard that Jesus was from Nazareth he said to Philip, "Can anything good come out of Nazareth?" (John 1:46). Jesus' geographical extraction showcases His humility.

Jesus identifies with His people not only by hailing from an insignificant city but also by undergoing the rite of baptism. Jesus underwent John's baptism of repentance which was for the remission of sins. Did Jesus need to have sins forgiven? No. But, as Paul writes, "He made Him who knew no sin to be sin for us, that we might become the righteousness of God in Him" (2 Cor. 5:21).

*Christ's Identification with God*
Jesus' baptism account is one of the great Trinitarian texts of the Bible. In Jesus' baptism the three distinct persons of the Godhead are shown to be intimately united. The Father speaks to the Son words of affirming love. The Spirit, in the form of a dove, publicly sets Him apart indicating that He is no ordinary man. As the Anointed One He is distinguished from all other people (cf. Is. 61:1) and equipped for a monumental task. How meaningful were those powerful words which pulsed through Christ's mind: "You are my beloved Son, in whom I am well pleased." Christ was about to begin a public ministry that would bring upon Him shame, hostility, powerful temptation to sin, death, and even hell. God urges obedience by reminding His Son of their intimate and blessed relationship. Jesus was baptized in the Father's love to prepare Him for a second baptism of the Father's wrath on Calvary (Luke 12:50).

If Christ's baptism was encouraging to Him, it is to believers as well. Christians always have the Spirit, but God uniquely prepares us for difficult tasks. Sometimes we are filled with fear to step out of ourselves for God. We need to remember that where God calls He also empowers. We also need to remember God's pattern as we urge others to greater faithfulness. He was not content to assume that His Son knew of His love. He knew that something powerful happens when we verbally affirm the love we have for others.

These words of the Father are also important words for how we view Christ. If the Father was not pleased with His Son, then we could not be saved. We are staking our lives on the sacrifice of Christ's own life which He offered to the

Father. If that life was not well pleasing to the Father, then we have no forgiveness. But we can have the confidence of knowing that Christ's sacrifice was accepted by God because He is His beloved Son. In fact, God says these same words to believing Christians. If you have repented of your sins and trusted in Christ as mediator, then the Father says to you today, "You are my beloved, adopted son or daughter, in whom I am well pleased." It is true that everything we do is stained with sin. But, as Paul affirms, "I am crucified with Christ; it is no longer I who live, but Christ lives in me; and the life which I now live in the flesh I live by faith in the Son of God, who loved me and gave Himself for me" (Gal. 2:20).

## Christ's Temptation (1:12–13)

Following His baptism, Jesus was three times tempted by Satan in a dry and solitary setting surrounded by wild beasts. The name "Satan" means "adversary." This is an appropriate introduction to the clash that Jesus initiated between Himself and the devil. In just a few short years this adversary would be defeated, though he will not be fully incapacitated until the last day.

We can understand only a little of how Jesus was tempted because we are so prone to give in to temptation and, therefore, rarely ever experience its full power. In football, quarterbacks can't afford to experience the full hit of the linemen so they often slide down when they are about to be hit. This is what you and I often do. The husband who is tempted to get angry at his wife fights the urge for a moment and then gives in. The man who is tempted to look at pornographic images on the computer might go a few days or weeks without looking but then gives in. A woman is tempted to share a shocking bit of gossip but gives in before the temptation even gets strong. We have never experienced the intensity of temptation which Christ experienced because we give in so quickly. "In your struggle against sin, you have not yet resisted to the point of shedding your blood" (Heb. 12:4, NIV). But Christ did!

Here is the comfort in Christ's temptation: *He did not give in.* As Christians we struggle sometimes with doubt. We grieve over our sins and wonder how we could possibly be saved. We lament over how easily we give in to temptation. We are terrified by our failures. In times like this we must take comfort in the temptation of Christ, *because He passed the test!* Your salvation does not depend on your performance but on Christ's. Here we have a grand demonstration that Christ will never fail us.

Jesus' temptation was heightened by His physical weakness. Matthew and Luke tell us He had nothing to eat during that time. Probably the longest that some of us have gone without food is less than one day. Think about how easily Esau gave up his birthright after a relatively brief fast. Christ hadn't eaten for forty days. Still He held fast to his birthright which becomes our blessing by faith in Him. Christ is contrasted with God's disobedient son, Israel, who wandered in the wilderness forty years (Num. 14:34). He is shown to be the true ark of salvation which was battered about a turbulent sea for forty days and nights (Gen. 7:12).

At the conclusion of this God-ordained time of testing, God the Father ministered to His Son through angels. The end of obedience is blessing.

In the first lesson we suggested three ways to engage Mark's Gospel in terms of application: What is Christ teaching? What kind of life does God bless or judge? What do we learn of God's redemptive work in Christ? The following chapters won't always outline these questions so explicitly, but to underscore the methodology, let's consider each in turn.

### What Is Christ Teaching?

In this passage Christ doesn't say anything; He utters no promises or commands. But God, in publicizing Christ's authority, *is* teaching us the importance of this question. Authority is a huge issue in teaching; just a few verses later, Mark tells how the people marveled over Jesus' authoritative teaching. If you don't have authority and credentials, what you say carries little weight. Why is it when a black-and-white car—with its lights flashing—races up behind your car, you pull over? You instantly recognize that the police officer in your rearview mirror has authority. In His baptism God broadcasts the absolute authority of His Son; in His temptation Christ proves His authority. Understandably, newly commissioned military officers fresh out of college struggle to command the same respect as seasoned and tested soldiers. In the wilderness Christ is tested and demonstrates His right to our respect and obedience.

### What Kind of Life Does God Bless or Curse?
God blesses the life of total commitment. How else could you describe the life of John the Baptist (Matt. 11:11)? But we also learn that God blesses the life of repentance. You will never outgrow sin in this life. But, by God's grace, you can develop a lifelong habit of "repentance leading to salvation" (2 Cor. 7:10).

### What Do We Learn About Christ's Redemptive Work?
God is fulfilling the promise made in the Old Testament that He would defeat Satan, and He's doing that through His beloved Son. In the garden of Eden the first Adam scurried away before the victorious devil (Gen. 3:8); in the wilderness of Judea, the devil limped away before the victorious second Adam (Luke 4:13).

Preparation is half the battle. After this preparation we have a pretty good sense of how the battle between Christ and Satan will end. This Gospel *is* good news! And keep in mind . . . this is only the beginning!

## Questions

1. What do you learn about Christ by reading Mark's opening Old Testament quotations in their original contexts?
2. How does John the Baptist glorify Christ?
3. How can we imitate John in glorifying Christ?
4. To what degree is your life characterized by confession of sins?
5. Why does the Father pronounce His love to Jesus at His baptism?
6. Is there anything about the Father's declaration that we can bring into our various relationships?
7. How does Christ's baptism convince us of His sympathy with and toward sinners?
8. Reflect on the fact that it was the Spirit who drove Jesus into the wilderness to test Him (Mark 1:12).
9. Why is Christ's temptation significant for the believer?

1. Calvin sees the beginning of John's preaching as "the abrogation of the law and the beginning of the gospel, strictly speaking" *Harmony of the Gospels* (Grand Rapids: Baker, 1989), 1:174.

2. Calvin, *Harmony of the Gospels,* 1:197. Calvin also maintains, in this connection, that Christian baptism today is the same as that which John administered.

3. Charles Erdman, *The Gospel of Mark* (Philadelphia: Westminster Press, 1945), 24.

# THE KINGDOM COMES

Mark 1:14–45

Maybe you know someone who takes a long time to get to the point in a conversation. Sometimes these are the same people who (after several minutes of not getting to the point) say, "to make a long story short . . ." but of course by then it's too late.

The writer of the second Gospel didn't have that problem. Mark's is the "action gospel" that focuses on the deeds of Christ. It shouldn't surprise us that after one introductory verse and twelve verses describing Christ's preparation for ministry, Mark gets right to the point, which for him is the public ministry of Jesus Christ. Jesus began His public ministry some time after John was thrown into prison. John had said, "He must increase, but I must decrease" (John 3:30). Now John's hope was being realized. The plan of God was unfolding according to divine schedule, as it always does, and as it is in your life right now.

Mark helps us to understand that Christ's ministry revolved around preaching, discipling, and healing, three activities of the Savior which God's children increasingly value as they gain deeper experience with Him.[1]

## Jesus' Preaching Ministry (1:14–15, 21–22, 35–39)

Jesus began His preaching in an important location, the synagogue (1:21, 39). Jesus' first mission was to redeem the lost sheep of Israel (Matt. 10:6; 15:24). After all, to them "pertains the adoption, the glory, the covenant, the giving of the law, the service of God, and the promises" (Rom. 9:4). For thousands of years God had been grooming the Jews to receive their Messiah. Now "the time is fulfilled" (Mark 1:15). All of the messianic arrows of the Old Testament are aimed at Jesus of Nazareth.

## The Priority of Jesus' Preaching

After being tested in the wilderness, the first thing Jesus did was preach the gospel. "Jesus came to Galilee, preaching the gospel of the kingdom of God, and saying, 'The time is fulfilled, and the kingdom of God is at hand. Repent, and believe in the gospel'" (1:14–15). Jesus later announced to His disciples that preaching was a chief reason why He came to earth (1:38). What a commentary on the importance of preaching!

The Bible teaches that preaching is the main vehicle of the Christian message (Rom. 10:14–15). And although the mission of the church isn't limited to preaching, churches must stay in step with Jesus in prioritizing the public declaration of the gospel. Churches demonstrate a high view of preaching by ensuring that other elements of worship never supplant the sermon. Churches must maintain a commitment to call gifted and godly ministers and to ensure that their preachers receive ongoing instruction and encouragement in their heralding task. Individuals within a congregation honor the priority Jesus gives to preaching by being mentally, spiritually, and physically prepared to receive the word from the pulpit as the Word of God (1 Thess. 2:13). Congregants who are serious about truly hearing God will engage the preaching both during and after the sermon.

Part of engaging the sermon means knowing what to listen for.

*The Content of Jesus' Preaching*

There are two main parts to Jesus' simple message. The first is an indicative statement, that is, a statement of what is: "The kingdom of God is at hand." The second is an imperative statement, that is, a statement of what should be done: "Repent and believe in the gospel" (v. 15). Biblical heralds help listeners understand the truth about important matters such as grace, sin, and the life to come; that's the indicative. But they also bring truth to bear on the listeners' wills by declaring their obligations; that's the imperative. As the master preacher, Jesus does both.

Jesus announces the reality that the kingdom is at hand (1:14–15) by saying at least four things about the arrival of the reign of God.[2] First, the kingdom physically came in the incarnation of Jesus. He is the king who is overturning the kingdom of darkness–and He is here! And though bodily absent, Christ is still ruling from heaven through His Spirit. Second, the kingdom gradually comes as hearts and lives are won over to God through the gospel. Third, the kingdom has structurally come as Christ builds His church on earth. Christ calls people to both a personal and communal relationship with Him. Fourth, the kingdom will universally come on the last day. The kingdom is both a present reality and a future expectation.

Jesus answers the important matter of how one becomes a citizen of this kingdom by issuing two imperatives: "Repent, and believe in the gospel." We could say that He demands a dual response to the preaching of the kingdom. First, Jesus commands: "Repent!" With this command, Jesus is not calling for a one-time expression of sorrow over sin. Rather, He calls sinners to "undergo a radical change of heart and life, a complete turnabout of life."[3] To repent is to grow increasingly dissatisfied with sin and to turn from it in disgust. Jesus' second command is to become increasingly satisfied with Him. To believe in the gospel is to know the good news that "not only to others, but to me also, remissions of sins, everlasting righteousness and salvation are freely given by God, merely of grace, only for the sake of Christ's merits."[4] To believe in the gospel doesn't merely mean to know it is true. It means to stake your life on its truth. I believe the gospel when I trust that Christ provides healing for my sin, remission for my guilt, and a gracious reward of heavenly glory.

### The Authority of Jesus' Preaching (1:22)[5]

Although Jesus preached quintessential good news, not everyone was impressed (cf. 2:7). Notably, however, everyone recognized that Jesus wasn't just sharing the opinions of men. They could tell that He spoke with a superhuman authority (v. 22). With unique suitability, Jesus' preaching was saturated with the Old Testament formula so commonly used by heavenly spokesmen: "Thus says the Lord." This is what true preaching always says. Martyn Lloyd Jones said that in preaching, "The hearer . . . knows that he has been dealt with and addressed by God through the preacher."[6] Of course, Jesus did so as no other can.

Still, Jesus did not do His preaching alone. In close connection with Jesus' preaching ministry was His discipling ministry.

## Jesus' Discipling Ministry (1:16–20)[7]

The Son of God chose to call disciples. Think about that. We might wonder, wouldn't it have been better if the Lord of glory would have worked His ministry of reconciliation alone? Couldn't He have done it better without the disciples misunderstanding His mission, putting their feet in their mouths, and getting in the way (cf. 8:33)? After all, don't things usually get messy when *we* involve other people? These concerns notwithstanding, Jesus chose to call disciples.

*Who Are the Disciples?*

Although the word isn't used in Mark 1, Jesus' followers were disciples, literally "students." Before they were called they were simple, ordinary men. Some were pious (John 1:47); others were not (Mark 2:13–17). Jesus' group of disciples consisted of both blue- and white-collar workers. In many ways they were no different from you and me; and for good reason.

In their unique callings the disciples are prototypical Christians; they are like mirrors in which we see our own weaknesses, and how God provides strength to follow Him.

*To What Were the Disciples Called?*

First, Jesus called the disciples to follow Him (1:17). The implication is that all else is left behind. They could not stay in their boats and follow Jesus at the same time. Amazingly, they immediately left their nets (v. 18) because God had opened their eyes, causing them to see infinite value in Jesus and His kingdom; they perceived that nothing they could desire could compare with Christ (Ps. 73:25). To this day, no one will forsake the world, take up his cross, and follow Christ unless that person sees Him as incomparably more valuable than everything else (Mark 8:34).

Second, Jesus called his disciples to be changed by Him. He says, "And I will make you *become* fishers of men" (v. 17). What these men were, here on the shores of the Sea of Galilee, was not what they would become. Are you planning to be changed in your pursuit of Christ? Are you willing to have your prejudices conquered? Are you prepared to undergo the painful transformation called sanctification (Rom. 12:2)? The Christian life is a constant becoming.

Third, Jesus called His disciples to become fishers of men (1:17). In calling the disciples away from their nets, Jesus wasn't diminishing their profession. Instead, He used their secular vocation as a powerful illustration of the call of discipleship. "You know how to fish for fish, now fish for people! Jesus might likewise have called Matthew—the tax collector—to now collect tithes of gratitude from God's people." When God converts a farmer, He calls him to cultivate godliness in himself and others. When He calls a carpenter, He calls him to build up the family of God. When people become followers of God, they become acutely interested in the salvation and sanctification of those who are yet swimming in a sea of despair.

## Jesus' Healing Ministry (1:21–34, 40–45)

Jesus came to preach and to disciple. But He also came to heal.

### Why Did Jesus Heal?

There are at least seven reasons why Jesus' healings are integral to His ministry. First, He healed to authenticate His divinity. Anyone can teach, but only God can perform healing miracles (2:9–12). Second, Jesus healed to substantiate preaching. Jesus' mercy ministry was not divorced from the ministry of the word. Third, Jesus healed to promote faith. Later, He told His Jewish critics: "Though you do not believe Me, believe the works, that you may know and believe that the Father is in Me, and I in Him" (John 10:38). Fourth, Jesus healed to gain favor with the people. Sometimes He warned people not to talk about the healings because He didn't want to become a sensation.[8] Still, His healing was highly regarded by many (Mark 1:37; 5:20) Fifth, Jesus healed to showcase His love (Mark 1:41, Matt. 9:36). All of His miracles were for the benefit of others.[9] Sixth, Jesus healed to demonstrate man's appalling need.[10] Just think about all we learn of human suffering and need for a healer through the healing accounts in the Gospels. Our understanding of our plight would be impoverished without them. Finally, Jesus healed to point to a day when all things will be made right. His earthly mercy ministry foreshadows a day when "God will wipe away every tear" from the eyes of His redeemed people. "And there shall be no more death, nor sorrow, nor crying. There shall be no more pain, for the former things have passed away" (Rev. 21:4).

*Examples of Jesus' Healing*

Jesus healed the demon possessed (1:21–28). Jesus' first healing miracle teaches the sobering reality that the great battles in this world are not fought against flesh and blood but against spiritual powers (Eph. 6:12). In a culture dominated by philosophical materialism, Christians still believe in the existence of ghosts or spirits. And because the Bible teaches about the danger of unclean spirits—the Bible says that unclean spirits torment their hosts (Luke 6:18; Acts 5:16)—Christians handle demonology soberly and not for the purpose of entertainment. At the same time, believers are not paralyzed by fear over the world of darkness. Christ has authority over the spirit world. In fact, this is why Christ came, as the demon asked: "Did you come to destroy us?" (Mark 1:24). The implied answer is yes (cf. 1 John 3:8). Even unclean spirits obey Him (1:27).

Jesus healed the sick. There are three examples in this chapter of Jesus' ministry to the sick. Each example highlights a component of Jesus' healing ministry. First, Jesus healed Peter's mother-in-law (vv. 29–31). This was a total healing. A remarkable detail is given in verse 31: After the woman was healed "she served them." I have heard people scorn the fact that Peter's mother-in-law served Jesus and His band of followers shortly after having been bedridden with a fever. "The woman was ill with a serious fever and isn't even allowed time to fully recover before returning to service?" But that's the point: she was fully recovered! She had no need to rest; Jesus had restored her!

Second, Jesus healed the multitudes (vv. 32–34). Here is a great healing. Too often beleaguered Christians limit, in their own minds at least, Christ's ability to heal. We give the impression that the Lord's arm has been shortened (Num. 11:23); that He no longer works wonders on a grand scale. God's word challenges the limitations which our little faith places on the power of God.

Third, Jesus healed the leper (vv. 40–45). This was a compassionate healing. If you've ever seen *Ben Hur,* you have a pretty good sense of how "untouchable" lepers were. They had their own communities where they could languish well apart from normal society. At one point in the movie, Judah Ben Hur is talking to Pilate after seeing where his "mother and . . . sister live what's left of their lives." He reminds Pilate that they have become "lepers and outcasts without hope!" Jesus ignored the societal demarcations of His day. He looked at the leper with compassion "and touched him" (1:41).

We need to grasp the humiliating truth that we are that leper. We do not have rotting skin but, by nature, we have rotting, stinking hearts that separate us from the holy society of God. But in His condescending love Christ comes to us and says, "I am willing to make you clean." One commentator says, "The whole of the gospel is here in a nutshell."[11]

The first hundred days in office have come to be seen as a harbinger of the remainder of a public servant's term. Think of Mark 1:14–45 as Christ's first hundred days in office as the servant of God. What will His ministry be about? It will be about preaching, discipling, and healing. If you had been around during Jesus' ministry, how would you have fit into His ministry? Are you submitting to the preaching of Christ? Are you being discipled? Are you being healed by Jesus? Do you bring your hurts, your sins, your frustrations to Christ and say, "I want to be cleaned"? To use Jesus' own phrase, "The kingdom of God is at hand." Jesus is calling us to enter in by repenting of our sins and believing in the gospel of Jesus Christ.

## Questions

1. Reflect on Jesus' statement "the kingdom of God is at hand." How can a robust understanding of God's kingdom affect our Christianity?
2. How does Jesus' call to His disciples to "follow me" inform our approach to discipleship?
3. How is Jesus' preaching authority reflected in Christian preaching today?
4. Why is it important to view biblical preaching as being authoritative?
5. Are there ways in which Christians take dark spiritual things too lightly today?
6. What does Jesus' healing ministry teach us about a ministry of mercy today?
7. How do you suppose Jesus' prayer ministry (v. 35) related to His preaching ministry (v. 38)?
8. Do we ever underestimate Jesus' compassion toward hurting sinners (see. v. 41)?

1. Christ also came to suffer and die for the sins of the elect, but Mark doesn't unveil Christ's suffering ministry until Mark 8, when Christ sets His face to Jerusalem.

2. This division (with the exception of the reference to the church) is from R. Alan Cole, *The Gospel According to Mark: An Introduction and Commentary* (Grand Rapids: Eerdmans, 1997), 112. Cf. William Hendriksen, *Exposition of the Gospel According to Mark*, New Testament Commentary (Grand Rapids: Baker, 1976), 56–57.

3. Hendriksen, *Mark*, 58.

4. *Heidelberg Catechism* answer 21, from the *Psalter Hymnal* (Grand Rapids: Publication Committee of the Christian Reformed Church, Inc. 1959), 25.

5. Hendriksen provides five additional ways in which Jesus' teaching differed from that of the scribes: truth not speculation, significance not trivialities, system not rambling, vivid illustration not dry lectures, love for listeners (*Mark,* 63).

6. *Preachers and Preaching* (Grand Rapids: Zondervan, 1972), 56.

7. More will be said regarding Jesus' call of the disciples in connection with Mark 2:13–17 and Mark 3:13–19.

8. Jesus seems to forbid men to freely publish His reputation until the time when God reveals to Peter just who Jesus is (Mark 8:29). See Cole, *Mark*, 116.

9. One exception is the miracle of the money in the fish's mouth, which allowed Jesus and Peter to pay the temple tax (Matt. 17:27).

10. Herbert Lockyer, *All of the Miracles of the Bible: The Supernatural in Scripture Its Scope and Significance* (Grand Rapids: Zondervan, 1961), 153.

11. Cole, *Mark*, 118.

# JESUS CLASHES WITH RELIGIOUS "EXPERTS"

————————————————▶ ● ◀————————————————

**Mark 2:1–3:6**

Thankfully it's not too often that you run into someone who loves conflict. Some of us would do almost anything to avoid conflict. And yet, conflict has its advantages. Specifically, conflict often produces clarity. It's hard to really understand someone until you've had a few clashes with him or her. Conflict has a tendency of sharpening views and helping us understand various positions. That's what happens in the many conflicts recorded in the Gospels. Jesus clashes with the religious elite; they criticize Him, He responds to their charges. The result is that Jesus and His mission shine through with greater brilliance.

Mark 2, and the first six verses of Mark 3, consists of four "clash" narratives that clarify, near the beginning of Jesus' ministry, what He came to do. In the process, "each of the four collisions in [these verses] reveals something radically inviting about Jesus."[1]

The objections raised in each case come from religious "experts," either scribes or Pharisees. The Pharisees were a religious sect whose name literally means "the separate ones." They separated themselves from the common folk whom they saw as beneath them. They were close students of the Scriptures; however, they added to them the traditions of men—which they kept scrupulously. They were also hypocrites in that they liked to show off their religiosity. The scribes were the professional students and teachers of the law. They are sometimes referred to as lawyers (Matt. 22:35) or rabbis (Matt. 23:6–8). Most of the scribes were Pharisees. Sadly, the scribes and Pharisees had departed from the simple, spiritual faith of the Bible and had reduced religion to legal formalism.[2] When religious formalists meet Jesus, conflict is inevitable.

We will look at these four clash narratives through the lens of a repeating pattern. First, we will try to paint a clear picture of the scene or context of the clash. Second, we will try to understand the objection that the religious leaders raised. Third, we will examine the response Jesus gave and the light it sheds on Him and His mission.

## Clash over Forgiveness of Sins (2:1–12)
*Painting the Scene*
Jesus began His ministry in Nazareth by preaching, discipling, and healing. The authority of His ministry became immediately obvious. Once the news of Jesus' power began to spread, He became very popular (for a while). In fact, His popularity prevented Him for a time from entering the cities (1:45).

Before long Jesus returned to a Galilean city called Capernaum. Upon his entering a house, people began to flock to Him for healing. One of those who needed healing was a paralyzed man. Because he couldn't walk he was carried to the house by his friends. But due to the crowd they couldn't get him and his bed close enough to Jesus. So they carried the paralytic up an outdoor stairway, removed some of the earth and plant material that made up the roof (Luke 5:19), and lowered him through. Jesus saw their faith and pronounced his sins forgiven.

Before moving to the objection, let's not miss how much these men loved their paralyzed friend and the length to which they went to bring him to Christ. Many of us have very good intentions toward the lost. But sometimes our good intentions are not combined with equal ambition. Ask yourself, "What will I do to bring the hurting to Christ?" The friends of this paralytic answered this question with tenacity!

*Objection: Why Does Jesus Claim to Forgive Sins?*
Like the rest of the questions, this is not a sincere quest for clarity. His critics were accusing Jesus of blasphemy, or speaking against God. After all, "Who can forgive sins but God?" Notice how they set themselves up for a fall. If only God can forgive sins, and if Jesus has been given power to forgive sins, He is God.

*Answer: Jesus Is Able to Forgive Sins Because He Is God*
Here is an example of Jesus healing to authenticate His message and His divinity. The sign of healing "demonstrate[s] that the Son of Man has power to forgive sins" (v. 10). The Pharisees have rightly reasoned that only God can forgive sins. In fact, that's why Jesus says, "Which is easier?" The answer seems to be "neither." Both are impossible for man. But with God all things are possible.

Jesus has the power to forgive sins. Are there sins in your life that you cannot overcome? Are there patterns of behavior that you hate and yet continue to do? Are there blots on your conscience that you cannot remove? Jesus alone has the power to forgive, or send away, sins. Go to Him and ask for forgiveness. And listen to Jesus say to you, through His word, "Your sins are forgiven." To forgive means "to cancel a debt." Unbelieving legalists dislike being indebted to Christ. But to God's children there is no greater reality.

## Clash over Associating with Sinners (2:13–17)
*Painting the Scene*
Some time later Jesus went out by the sea and began to teach the multitudes. Passing by He saw a tax collector named

Matthew (his Greek name; Levi is his Hebrew name) and called him to be His disciple. Matthew got up to follow and in his joy invited Christ to dine with him and his friends. As the old saying goes, "Birds of a feather flock together." So it was with Matthew. Like him, his friends were tax collectors and "sinners."

The term "sinner" is interesting. On the one hand this was a label that the Pharisees applied to anyone who didn't observe the law like they did. The term especially fit hated tax collectors who worked for the Romans. On the other hand, the friends of Matthew with whom Jesus dined were real sinners. They weren't simply those whom the Pharisees didn't accept, but sinners in the sight of God. Matthew's friends lived corrupt lives. They were cheats, swearers, fornicators, and drunks. They were the types of people that you and I might be embarrassed to be seen with.

*Objection: Why Does Jesus Associate with Sinners?*
Again, this is not a sincere question but an indictment against the character of Jesus. What they are saying is, "The Messiah, the king of righteousness, would never associate with such sinners."

*Answer: Jesus Came to Call Sinners to Repentance*
Jesus' answer is one of the most hope-giving texts in Scripture. He associates with them because they are such sinners! Jesus came to earth as the Great Physician to heal those who were sick unto death with sin (1 Tim. 1:15). Jesus came as the great friend of sinners (Matt. 11:19).

This raises a practical question: "Should Christians be friends with sinners?" To answer this question, we need to first assess evangelistic opportunities with both eyes open. The proverb "Evil company corrupts good habits" doesn't forbid engagements with unbelievers, but it does sound a note of caution. When we wrestle against flesh and blood we must do so clad in the whole armor of God, "being watchful" (Eph. 6:12–18). Second, those who are serious about engaging sinners should check their intentions. There was a purpose in Jesus' friendship. He was committed to demonstrating the gospel to sinners. He loved them. He called them to repent. We need to love the world on God's terms, not on the world's terms.

The Pharisees caught only half of God's program for sinners. They liked God's warnings not to blithely associate with the ungodly (e.g., Ps. 1:1). But they missed His expectation that His people would teach transgressors God's ways that sinners should be converted to Him (Ps. 51:13; cf. Ps. 25:8). Like the Pharisees, we run the risk of "arranging our lives so that we are with non-believers as little as possible." But "the Christian life is not to be one of *isolation* nor *assimilation*, but *mission*."3

## Clash over Fasting (2:18–22)

*Painting the Scene*

The next clash took place over the issue of fasting. Specifically, the disciples of John the Baptist and of the Pharisees were fasting. They wondered, condescendingly it seems, why the disciples of Christ failed to fast as they did.

*Objection: Why Does Jesus Not Fast?*

In three of the clashes described in this narrative, the scribes and Pharisees accused Jesus of sins of commission. When it comes to fasting the accusation was over a perceived sin of omission. The disciples of John and of the Pharisees criticized Jesus' disciples by pointing out their own performance: "Look at us! We're fasting. Why aren't you?" Mark implicitly points out that the Pharisees took a wrong approach to fasting. God required that those who fast should not broadcast their piety (Isa. 58:5; cf. Matt. 6:16–18). The Bible does not demand that fasting be done in absolute secrecy, but it does require that one fast without a spirit of pretentiousness.

*Answer: Jesus Transforms Fasting*

This is Jesus' longest and most complex answer. He gives two distinct answers to the Pharisees' question. First, He explains that there is no fasting while the groom is present (2:19–20). This answer makes sense if we understand what fasting is. Fasting is an act of devotion in which one voluntarily and temporarily deprives himself of food or other pleasures or necessities. Through fasting believers "are humbled before God, and withdraw from the flesh those things with which it is cherished, to the end that it may the more willingly and easily obey the Spirit . . . Fasting is a help to the prayers of the saints and all virtues."[4] We need to be clear: Jesus is not speaking against fasting. In the Sermon on the Mount, Jesus commends fasting as a regular component of the Christian life (Matt. 6:17). Jesus is simply saying that fasting would not be appropriate at a wedding like it would be at a funeral. His coming cemented a marriage between God and His children, though until the wedding feast of heaven we will endure many funereal moments. Fasting would not be appropriate at a wedding like it would be at a funeral. In the Christian life there will be alternating seasons of joy and thanksgiving; sadness and fasting.

Jesus' second answer explains why His disciples should not fast as do the Pharisees. When He talks about old and new cloth and old and new wineskins, He insists that the new is not compatible with the old (2:21–22). When Jesus came He brought something new. In Him the kingdom of God is at hand. If you miss Jesus, then you are part of an obsolete religion. That's what became of the Jewish leaders. The Pharisees were living joyless, man-centered lives because they were outside of the kingdom. Jesus brings a fullness to life, not an emptiness. And that's why His disciples were intentionally not fasting, to paint a contrast between their religion and that of the Pharisees.

## Clash over Working on the Sabbath (2:23–3:6)

*Painting the Scene*

There are two scenes in this clash in which most of us fail to see any scandal whatsoever. This is because we can hardly relate to how even the godly Jews of Jesus' day approached the day of rest and worship. We have an even harder time understanding the straitjacket approach which the Pharisees took to the Sabbath.

In the first narrative Jesus and His disciples were walking through a grain field. When they began to feel hungry, they plucked some grain and had a snack while they walked. You've done something like this when you stopped to pick a few blackberries on a hike in the woods.

In the second narrative, Jesus healed a man with a withered hand on the Sabbath.

*Objection: Why Does Jesus Violate the Sabbath Day?*

The Pharisees thought that the disciples' eating and Jesus' healing were offensive to God. This is so because they had adopted a largely negative view of the Sabbath; the Sabbath is a day of "thou shalt nots." From the start, we see a perverted theology. Granted, there are restrictions placed upon Sabbath activity, but this is one of only two of the Ten Commandments that is stated in the positive: "Remember to keep the Sabbath day holy!"

*Answer: Jesus Is Lord of the Sabbath*

Jesus' answer comes in three parts. First, Jesus did not violate the Sabbath but merely the Pharisees' understanding of it. This is a helpful principle. We are not bound to observe the Lord's Day the same way as everyone else simply because that's the way they do it. Nor can we expect others to honor God's special day exactly as we do.

Second, Jesus defends Himself and His disciples by announcing His authority. Jesus is the Lord of the Sabbath;

it's His day. Imagine if someone visited your house and as you reached toward a bowl of fruit to grab an apple, he cried out, "Why are you eating that apple? Who said you could have it?" You would probably say, "This is my house, my apple. I don't need permission." Christ wasn't answerable to the Pharisees; they were answerable to Him. So are we. The Christian Sunday is the Lord's Day. Do we treat Sunday as our day or as the Lord's?

Third, Jesus did what was right on the Lord's Day. He engaged in works of necessity (eating), in works of mercy (healing), and in works of worship. The Lord's Day is the right day to do works that anticipate an eternity with God.

In two of the clash narratives Mark tells the reaction of at least part of the crowd. "Then the Pharisees went out and immediately plotted with the Herodians against him, how they might destroy him" (3:6). The Pharisees demonstrated a spirit of judgmentalism and unbelief. When the paralytic was healed, they were critical. When sinners were loved, they were smug. When the bridegroom stood before them, they exalted themselves in self-righteousness. When Christ fulfilled the Sabbath, they debated about tradition. Can you see some faint (or not so faint) reflection of yourself in them?

By contrast, after the healing of the paralytic, we read: "All were amazed and glorified God, saying, 'We never saw anything like this!'" (2:12). In fact, Luke adds that the former paralytic went home "glorifying God" (Luke 5:25). They saw the glory of God in Jesus Christ, and it changed their outlook on life.

Every time we hear God's Word we have a clash with Jesus. Every glimpse at God's glory changes our outlook. After every sermon we see our sin either more or less sharply. After every Bible reading we see Jesus as more or less sufficient for our needs. From Lord's Day to Lord's Day we are either more or less invigorated to live rightly before His face. How have you clashed with Jesus today?

## Questions

1. Can you identify someone in your life whom you should prayerfully attempt to bring to Jesus (cf. Mark 2:3–4)?
2. Do we need to be more courageous in "eating with tax collectors and sinners" (Mark 2:16)?
3. What approach or cautions should we take in engaging sinners?
4. Is it possible that we have overlooked the importance of fasting because of its abuses, some of which we read about in the Gospels?
5. How is Jesus like new wine (Mark 2:22)?
6. In what ways might we demonstrate pharisaical attitudes toward the Lord's Day?
7. Do we treat Sunday as our day or as the Lord's?
8. Strictly speaking, Jesus didn't "save life" when He healed the man with the withered hand. Still, how is this an appropriate expression of what He did and what we are called to do?
9. How have you clashed with Jesus today?

1. Kent Hughes, *Mark: Jesus, Servant and Savior*, 2 vols., Preaching the Word (Westchester, IL: Crossway, 1989), 1:75.

2. James Orr, ed., *International Standard Bible Encyclopedia* (Grand Rapids: Eerdmans, 1952), s.v. "Scribes," by Frank Hirsch.

3. Hughes, *Mark,* 1.71, 72

4. *Second Helvetic Confession* 24.4, from Joel Beeke and Sinclair Ferguson, eds., *Reformed Confessions Harmonized* (Grand Rapids: Baker Books, 1999), 174.

# DRAWING UP LINES!

---

**Mark 3:7–35**

In 1858 Abraham Lincoln gave one of the most important speeches of his career, his "house divided" speech.[1] Quoting Jesus' words in Mark 3, Lincoln drew a line in the sand. America could not continue to be half-free and half-slave. At some point the house would no longer be divided; its loyalty would go one way or the other.

Mark has already described Jesus' clashes with the scribes and Pharisees, those experts of an earth-bound religion. In Mark 3 the division between the kingdom of God and the kingdom of man comes into sharper focus as Jesus begins to draw crowds, call kingdom officers, and identify the primary mark of those who are members of His kingdom. Mark is using these narratives to help us hear Jesus ask vital questions. On which side are you? Are you part of the crowd or are you a disciple? Is Jesus just a good man or is He your Lord?

## Jesus Draws a Crowd (3:7–12)

After clashing with the scribes and Pharisees, Jesus withdrew with His disciples and began attracting a great multitude (3:7). Already His promise from the previous chapter is ringing true: "I did not come to call the righteous, but sinners, to repentance" (2:17). When Jesus left Capernaum it's as if He was saying, "The religious people here are already righteous, in their own eyes at least. But My message will resonate with real sinners." Before long, sinners began following Jesus in droves! Reports of Jesus' miraculous works and message of restoration spread rapidly among the physically needy and spiritually underfed sheep of Israel.

*Jesus Cares for the Crowd*
Before long, however, the large crowd, with the energy of an agitated sea, began to take on a life of its own. Sometimes we imagine Jesus calmly and casually walking through swaying meadows, dispensing truth to disciplined students who hung on His every word. In reality this scene was chaotic! People in the unwieldy crowd bumped against Jesus, probably stepping on His feet, and interrupting His speech with their questions and requests; the noise must have been tremendous (3:9; cf. v. 20). To avoid being crushed, Jesus asked His disciples to keep a small boat just off shore as an emergency exit from the crowds.

Does this scene remind you of your own life? Ever feel like your life is a transition from one chaotic scene to the next? Never forget: "We do not have a High Priest who cannot sympathize with our weaknesses, but was in all points tempted as we are, yet without sin" (Heb. 4:15). As a sympathetic high priest Jesus can relate even to being pulled in a hundred directions at once. He is the Savior of the stressed-out, the beat-up, and the overworked. Jesus can rightly call the weary to Himself because He experienced intense weariness securing our redemption.

From the vortex of this swirling mass of humanity Jesus steadily ministered to one broken life after another, healing both the physically afflicted and the spiritually burdened. Mark tells us that the unclean spirits "fell down before [Jesus] and cried out, saying, 'You are the Son of God'" (3:11). So saying, the unclean spirits pronounce one of the clearest confessions of the deity of Christ in Mark's Gospel so far. Curiously, in response, Jesus "sternly warned them that they should not make him known" (v. 12). It's hard for us to understand this, but Jesus is not desperate for publicity. The contemporary church is plagued with the false notion that ministry happens by publicizing Jesus without qualification. But in truth, Jesus is looking to be promoted by men and women who love Him and seek to honor Him, not by demons who want to destroy Him or, as the case often is today, by crass marketing techniques. Jesus is drawing a line in the sand. He's saying, "Those who love Me may and must confess Me. Everyone else should keep quiet."

## Jesus Retreats from the Crowd

It's no surprise that after this chaotic scene, Jesus retreats to a more peaceful setting. Our Savior willingly shouldered massive burdens, but He also respected His humanity by engaging pressure with wisdom. According to Luke 6:12–16, Jesus went up on the mountain to pray. In fact, "all night he continued in prayer to God." Jesus combatted pressure by communing with His heavenly Father. Sometimes we get so busy that we fall out of regular fellowship with God and with His people. Instead, we need to get in the habit of turning to God in prayer exactly when the pressures are mounting. When we think we're too busy to pray, we're too busy *not* to pray. We also need to be wise about our limits. Jesus experienced the temptation of busyness without sinning. But like Him we are tempted to be people-pleasers instead of God-pleasers. We are tempted to focus on output and performance rather than on the overall well-being of ourselves and our families. Too often we are energized by visions of our glory, not God's. This same Jesus is still praying for the weary. We must take the time to seek help from our praying high priest.[2]

After a night of prayer, Jesus continued to build His kingdom by calling kingdom officers, also known as disciples.

## Jesus Calls His Disciples (3:13–19)

The calling of the disciples needs to be understood within the motif of the kingdom. Jesus is appointing officers of that structural manifestation of the kingdom of God on earth, the church. He, therefore, appoints twelve "as a symbol of the fact that he was building the 'new Israel' out of the old."[3] By way of anticipation and application, church elders today—despite their many limitations—are not just board members, they are kingdom leaders. God's officers, ancient and contemporary, are—believe it or not—the ones "he himself wanted" (3:13). Many of the disciples had serious character flaws, and one of those whom He chose was a reprobate (John 17:12). What a demonstration of the sovereign providence of God! He is building His kingdom in ways that are so far above ours. Christ handpicked the man who would betray Him to death. God is fully in charge of everything, even those means by which evil comes (cf. Amos 3:6). Only when we come to peace with God's absolute sovereignty will we be able to rest in His decisions and begin to live a contented life, whether we are called to lead or to follow.

Mark identifies three reasons why Jesus chose these first kingdom leaders. First, Jesus called disciples "to be with him" (v. 12), a decision that certainly casts light on His authentic humanity. In the words of an ancient hymnist, Jesus is "of th' eternal Father true and only Son | Manhood to deliver, manhood didst put on."[4] Manhood flourishes in community. As a real man Jesus had a need for companionship, just as He had a need for food and rest. Jesus, therefore, called twelve friends (John 15:15) to be with Him, and He drew three of the twelve (Peter, James, and John) into His inner circle. We too need to genuinely share life with others who can encourage and energize us, people to whom we reach out and upon whom we can learn to depend.[5]

But, spending time with these twelve was also integral to Jesus' plan for training His kingdom leaders. Is it possible that we sometimes miss Jesus' simple approach to discipleship? Discipleship is less a system by which we train ourselves to be spiritual, and more about genuine fellowship with Jesus. Christ promises to always be with His people (Matt. 28:20), and there are various ways in which we experience His presence. But, all of our fellowship experiences are informed and fueled through personal, family, and especially corporate worship. The more we commune with Jesus in true worship, the more evident it will be that we have been with Him (cf. Acts 4:13). Going through religious motions never conformed anyone to Christ; being with Him through believing fellowship always does.

Second, Jesus called disciples to send them out to preach.[6] While the twelve disciples were kingdom heralds in a unique and unrepeatable way, their preaching ministry at least hints at one of the basic reasons God still draws followers, namely, to broadcast His fame. As Jesus will make plain (6:19), housewives, factory workers, students, as well as preachers, have an unshakable calling to tell others what God has done for them in Christ. If you are a disciple of Jesus and truly know whom you have believed (2 Tim. 1:12), the purpose of your life is to point others to the singular beauty of the Savior.

Third, Jesus called disciples to heal sicknesses and to cast out demons. The disciples' healing ministry was a sign that God had indeed bound the strong man Satan and was plundering his house (3:27), and a seal that God had anointed His disciples as His ambassadors. In this sense the apostles occupy a unique position in the history of God's redemption. Paul speaks of "signs, wonders and mighty deeds" as "signs of the apostles" (2 Cor. 12:12). Still, apostles do model for us the important role all God's children play as channels of His mercy. Every believer can think creatively about how to demonstrate God's care for both body and soul. In the words of Jesus, we can all offer a cup of cold water in His name (Matt. 10:42).

Jesus couldn't have called His disciples at a better time, because in the next passage, He is sharply attacked.

## Jesus Endures Hostility (3:20–30)

The attack against Jesus came in two waves. First, His family came to retrieve Him believing Him to be out of His mind (v. 21). In their unrepentant and unconverted state (John 7:5) they thought that He was a religious fanatic. He wasn't eating (Mark 3:20) or sleeping well. Instead He had thrown himself into preaching and healing the multitudes. "Had He," they wondered, "in His religious zeal thrown away His mind?"

Most people will tolerate a little religion, but as soon as your religious convictions start to drive your life, people get uncomfortable. This is a method Satan uses to keep Christians ineffective. He says, "Don't allow your faith to determine how you engage mass media, or which school you will go to, or which friends you will keep, or who you will marry." The apostle Paul had one of the sharpest minds in the ancient world, yet he admitted that from a worldly point of view he was out of his mind for the sake of God (2 Cor. 5:13, NIV). Christians must be thinkers; we don't throw away our brains when we become believers. But we should take it as a compliment when people think we are out of our minds in our pursuit of godliness.

Second, the scribes accused Jesus of being possessed by an evil spirit. The scribes have changed their approach. In the previous chapter each of their accusations were at least grammatically cloaked as questions. This time the cloak is removed and they directly charge Jesus with being a demoniac. They insist that His powers came from below, not from above.

Jesus responded to this accusation in three ways. He first said that a house divided cannot stand (23–26). In a sense, Jesus is mocking the logic of the scribes. He's saying, "If I'm casting out demons by a demon then I am self-destructing."

Jesus' power clearly did not come from the devil. Second, Jesus said that the only way He could cast out demons is if He had bound the prince of demons, the devil. The Bible teaches that Jesus came to destroy the devil (Heb. 2:14). Satan does not have free reign in this world. We shouldn't ascribe too much power to him. Third, He warned them against committing the unpardonable sin. They were calling the Spirit of Jesus evil; sinning against the Spirit. There are several opinions about what the unpardonable sin is, but it is safe to say that the unpardonable sin is a continuous resistance of the Holy Spirit's ministry.

Jesus is drawing a line in the sand: "In which kingdom are you: the kingdom of the bound strong man or the kingdom of the one who bound him? Will you resist the Holy Spirit or submit to Him?"

## Jesus' True Family (3:31–35)

In this last narrative Jesus continues drawing a line between those who are for Him and those who are against Him. He uses an event involving His own biological family to illustrate this amazing truth: In building a kingdom, God is also growing a family. Christ's brothers, sisters, and mothers are those who pledge allegiance to the God of Scripture. They "love the Lord, [have a] heartfelt desire to serve Him according to His Word, to forsake the world, to mortify [their] old nature, and to lead a godly life."[7]

Don't overlook the fact that Jesus begins His teaching on the nature of the family of God by asking a question: "Who is my mother, or my brothers?" (v. 34). Questions are meant to challenge assumptions and promote thoughtful evaluation. The Reformed confessions list marks that help to identify true Christians, such as faith, righteousness, and love for God and neighbor. We are to use these marks to examine and test ourselves (2 Cor. 13:5), but to do so in light of the grace of God as He comforts us in our weaknesses. The mark of obedience "is not to be understood as if there did not remain in [Christians] great infirmities; but they fight against them through the Spirit all the days of their life, continually taking their refuge in the blood, death, passion, and obedience of our Lord Jesus Christ, in whom they have remission of sins, through faith in Him."[8] When Jesus came preaching the gospel of the kingdom He did not say, "The kingdom of God is at hand, therefore keep all God's laws perfectly, and you will be a member of this kingdom." Instead, He said, "Repent and believe." Christ is the believer's only hope, in seasons of success and in seasons that call for repentance.

Jesus' promotion of a new family of God also has implications for our fellowship. Those in Christ form a new family, complete with both blessings and responsibilities.[9] In the church believers treat older men as fathers, younger men as brothers, older women as mothers, younger women as sisters (1 Tim. 5:1–2). Believers have no permanent ties to anyone who isn't united to Christ by a living faith. At the same time, Jesus doesn't undermine the importance of the nuclear family, regardless of the faith commitments of its members. Mark is not suggesting that Jesus ignored His family or disowned them. Cults teach that your church is your only family. Jesus is more balanced. Paul goes so far as to say that one who does not provide for his household "has denied the faith and is worse than an unbeliever" (1 Tim. 5:8).

In this chapter Mark highlights three opinions of Jesus. Some thought He was out of His mind. Others said He was demon possessed. Ironically, the unclean spirits got it right: "You are the Son of God!" C. S. Lewis has masterfully and famously explained that these are the only three options regarding who Jesus is. People want to say that Jesus was simply a good moral teacher. But He didn't claim to be only a good moral teacher. He claimed to bring a kingdom that required repentance and faith. He believed that His life and ministry would change the world. If He was not really God, then He was out of His mind. The fact that Jesus claimed to be God means—if He really wasn't—that Jesus was no good moral teacher but a liar and a demon.[10]

Do not waver between two opinions. Jesus is Lord. Submit to His lordship today and cross that line from the kingdom of darkness into the kingdom of His light.

## Questions

1. Jesus is far more than our moral example. But is there any way in which we must emulate Christ's withdrawing from the crowds (Mark 3:7; cf. 1 Cor. 11:1)?

2. How do Christ's actions in Mark 3:9–10 warrant your worship?

3. What comfort can be derived from the fact that, regarding the disciples, Jesus "called to Him those He Himself wanted" (Mark 3:13)?

4. How are you comforted by Jesus' power over sickness and demons (Mark 3:15)?

5. The disciples were sent out to preach (Mark 3:14). What might that fact mean for those who are called to listen?

6. What does Jesus' concern for the physical welfare of those to whom His disciples preached mean for us today?

7. How should Jesus' claim to have bound Satan (Mark 3:27) affect our outlook on life?

8. In what ways could you and your group, as members of Christ's church, function more like a family?

9. Are there ways in which a church should not resemble a family?

1. June 16, 1858.
2. See *Heidelberg Catechism*, Q&A 116.
3. Sinclair Ferguson, *Let's Study Mark* (Edinburgh: Banner of Truth Trust, 2002), 41.
4. *Psalter Hymnal* (Grand Rapids: Publication Committee of the Christian Reformed Church, 1976), song number 363.
5. See Kent Hughes, *Disciplines of a Godly Man* (Wheaton, IL: Crossway, 1991), 57–67.
6. The preaching and healing ministry of the disciples will be considered in greater depth in connection with Mark 6 (vv. 12–13) and 9 (vv. 28–29).
7. Answer to question three of the Form for the Public Profession of Faith, *Psalter Hymnal* (Grand Rapids: Publication Committee of the Christian Reformed Church, 1959), 88.
8. *Belgic Confession*, Article 29.
9. See William Boekestein, "Christian Community: Seeking Contentment without Complacency," *Evangelical Times,* June 2013, 13.
10. C. S. Lewis, *Mere Christianity* (London: Collins, 1952), 54–56.

# HE TAUGHT IN PARABLES

———————————————▶ ● ◀———————————————

**Mark 4:1–34**

In 1990 General Motors purchased rights to a song performed by Bob Seger to use as a product theme.[1] Seger's song, "Like a Rock," become the motto for Chevy trucks for the next decade. The theme made a powerful impression in the minds of consumers. For right or wrong, people began to associate Chevy trucks with permanence and durability. Those three words, "like a rock," create a clear picture, and when applied to a vehicle they tell us exactly what the manufacturer wants us to think about it.

Parables function in a similar way; they impress upon the minds of the hearers the point being taught. In fact, Jesus begins two parables in Mark 4 by saying, "The kingdom of God is like . . ." Not like a rock, but like a farmer who sows his field, and like a mustard seed. It is critical to understand what parables are and how they function in order to understand the three parables in Mark 4.

## What Are Parables? (4:1–2, 9–13, 33–34)

A parable is a teaching method (4:2) by which one paints a picture to create a simple likeness of a deeper reality (4:30). Literally, a parable throws a lesson alongside of life (the Greek word *para* means "alongside of"; *bole* means "to throw"). Parables vividly describe a scene so that the listener can say, "I can picture that." Or, to use another analogy, a parable creates a window that allows us to view a concept from another angle. The traditional, simple definition of a parable is helpful (if not perfect): An earthly story with a heavenly meaning.

*How Parables Work*

Contrary to conventional wisdom Jesus told parables both to reveal and to conceal the mystery of the kingdom (4:10–13; 33, 34; cf. Matt. 13:10–17). The word "mystery" (4:11) indicates something that is not evident by intuition; not everyone understands. That's true of the kingdom of God; it's a mystery that must be revealed. By way of parables God makes some "get it" and leaves others in their own confusion. This dual purpose of parables is evident in Mark 4. The parables made a powerful impression on the disciples when they were made to understand them. Others found the parables confusing. Both results conformed to God's purpose. All the words of God serve a dual purpose; they both harden and soften.

Whether people understand it or not, a parable is a story designed to make a point and usually one main point. The various details of the story might not have meaning when isolated from the whole. The following would be an inappropriate way of isolating a detail from a parable: "Jesus said that the kingdom of God is like a mustard seed. Mustard is spicy. This parable teaches us the need for kingdom zest." Like all good stories, Jesus includes some details simply to support the story. On other occasions, the details are essential to the parable. In the parable of the sower, the sower helps us understand the role of a gospel minister (1 Cor. 3:5); the title of the main character is a vital detail. But, unless we have good reason to focus on the details we should stick to the main point.

*General Lessons from the Parables*

First, Jesus' parables teach us that God is a revealer. God reveals His invisible attributes by what He has made—this we call general revelation (Rom. 1:20). He also reveals Himself through the spoken word of special revelation. Jesus' teaching ministry is a powerful testimony to God's mission to reveal Himself to lost sinners. Jesus used a variety of means to communicate His truth, including questions, pictures, looks, gestures, actions, lectures, and stories. He taught in public and in private; in hostile and in cordial settings. In Mark 4 He taught from a boat. Why? Because that was how He could best reach the people who needed to hear His message. Jesus' parables are not always simple. But He does interpret the parables for those who will hear them (4:10). If we don't hear God's revelation, the problem is ours, not His (Rom. 1:18–24).

Second, Jesus' parables teach us that God is not obligated to reveal Himself to anyone.[2] God would be just to leave all of us in the darkness of our own wicked imaginations. Until we understand the terribleness of sin we will tend to think that God owes saving revelation to everyone. But to think this way would be hypocritical. We don't tell important secrets to our enemies but to our friends. Jesus uses parables to tell the mysteries of the kingdom to His friends, to those who have been given ears to hear and hearts to understand. The fact that He reveals Himself to anyone is an act of pure grace flowing from His sovereign election.

Third, Jesus' parables teach us to beware of hardening hearts. Through parables Christ speaks passionately to people whose hearts have grown dull of hearing (Matt. 13:13–15). Remember that the Pharisees and scribes had responded to Jesus' ministry with questions, doubts, and accusations; they have made it clear that they are outside of the kingdom. They've grown dull. Similarly, the crowds were largely following Jesus for amusement; they were not interested in the things of God. To these, therefore, Jesus spoke in parables to conceal from the profane God's precious things. Those who reject the clear teaching of God's Word will have it taken away from them (see Ezek. 7:26). Those, for example, who in their youth hear the gospel with disinterest can develop dull hearts which become seemingly impenetrable to spiritual things. Whatever they later hear of God might sound like confusing parables.

## Three Agricultural Parables

The basic point of each of the parables in Mark 4 is that the kingdom grows as the Word of God takes root in our hearts and lives.

*The Parable of the Four Soils (4:3–9, 13–20)*
In His first recorded parable, Jesus says that there are only two kinds of responders to the preaching of the Word. Those who hear either bear fruit, or they do not.[3] In the hand of a sower, a seed has one purpose: to bear fruit. Failure to do so betrays a problem in the soil, not the seed.

Jesus says there are two main types of non-fruit-bearing hearers, both of which have problems of the heart. The first type immediately rejects the seed of the Word. They are unresponsive and uninterested in the Word of God from the start. Jesus says these people are in bondage to Satan.[4] Perhaps you've tried to sow seed in this kind of heart. It seems hopeless. Be encouraged to keep spreading seeds. All it takes is God to hold Satan back and cause that seed to take root and grow, and they too will be saved.

Other fruitless hearers seem to receive the Word only to fall away. Some seem to be believers for a time but then apostatize; the gospel never developed sustainable roots in their lives. These hearers often fall away on account of the challenges of godliness. Sadly, into this category of hearers fell the masses of Jesus' audience. Thousands thronged our

Lord when He was new and popular, but when persecution came the crowds vanished. God promises a tremendous reward of grace. But the way to heaven is hard. Christ calls us to count the cost and take up the cross. If we don't, we'll fall away when the going gets tough.

Other hearers fall away on account of worldliness. In any square foot of earth there is only enough opportunity for so many things to grow. To the worldly the cares of the present age are stronger than the promise of the gospel. Is it possible that masses of people today are choking out the gospel's message by way of a steady distracting stream of mass media? Is not the myth of "wealth brings happiness" alive among us? Is there not a deceptive urge in each of us to gravitate toward that which gratifies our desires? How shall we interpret the swelling attendance rolls of churches where the gospel is light or absent but church is fun, the speaker charismatic, and programs abound? William Hendriksen calls them "preoccupied hearts" who are distracted from the gospel by worldliness, wealth, and wants. They have "no room for calm and earnest meditation on the word or message of the Lord."[5] Each of us should pray for deliverance from such distractions.

Gladly, there are also those who hear the Word and embrace it till the end. Mark 4:20 says three things about this last category of listeners.[6] First, fruit bearers hear the Word. We will not bear fruit unless we hear God speak (cf. Rom. 10:17). All of us are obligated to carefully listen to God speaking in the church, in family worship, and in private worship. When we add up the amount of time we spend hearing the Word of God on a given week, how does it compare with the time than we spend manicuring our nails or our yards? Are we hearing the Word?

Second, fruit bearers accept or receive the Word. The word for "accept" is elsewhere translated "welcome" (Acts 15:4, ESV). Those who are blessed by the Word welcome it. They don't see Bible reading or sermon listening as a duty to be done but as a gift to be received. Those who ultimately bear fruit also have a sensitivity to the Word; they accept what it says. They see themselves in subjection to the Word. They are often cut to the heart by it; they are convicted by it (Acts 2:37).

Third, fruit bearers apply the Word. Bearing fruit means putting the Word to work; it means using it the way God intended it to be used (2 Tim. 3:15–16). There are many who hear the Word, and even agree with it, but are unwilling to be changed by it and put it to work in their lives. One of the best ways to ensure that we apply the Word is to listen to it with application in mind. Whenever you hear something that pointedly speaks to you, acknowledge the convictions that you feel. Better yet, write down these convictions either in the form of a prayer ("God help me to . . .") or in the form of an indicative statement ("God wants me to . . ."). Sermon listening should be active, not passive. What kind of heart do you have? Are you receptive to the Word (Mark 4:9)?

### The Parable of the Growing Seed (4:26–29)

It's hard to miss that Jesus' first parables all have to do with seeds. The imagery of seed is well suited to emphasize at the same time God's sovereignty and man's responsibility.[7] As Paul says, man plants and waters but God brings the seed to fruition (1 Cor. 3:7). Both this and the next parable have to do with the growth of the kingdom. The main point of this parable is that the kingdom of God grows almost mysteriously toward a harvest. Even in a scientific age it is amazing to watch a seed grow from the earth with no human help.

Jesus told the parable of the growing seed to encourage His disciples. They were to proclaim the kingdom of God by preaching and healing. Yet, they were average men who were prone to fear and discouragement. Jesus assures us that where the gospel has taken root it will grow. We don't always know how. Sometimes we don't see the kingdom grow. We listen to the Word of God week after week, yet we feel stagnant. We pray, we preach, we invite our community to worship, yet we see no church growth. So it is when you watch a garden. Day after day you check and nothing happens. But before long growth is undeniable. As James writes, we need to be as patient as the farmer who waits for the precious fruit of the earth (James 5:7–8). As we trust God He will provide the increase (2 Cor. 9:10). Sometimes we wonder how a seed can grow where it does: I once saw a full-grown tomato plant growing in the crack of the sidewalk in front of a local pizzeria. When the kingdom grows within us or around us we should acknowledge that miracle and praise God for it. To the praise of God's glory, the kingdom will advance despite our failures because it is *God's* kingdom.

### The Parable of the Mustard Seed (4:30–32)

The final parable in this section has to do with one of the smallest of all garden seeds. Mustard seeds can be as small as one millimeter in diameter but can grow to twice the height of a man. Likewise, the kingdom begins small but will grow to great proportions (cf. 1 Kings 18:44–45). Jesus is reminding His audience of promises made in the Old Testament about Himself; a shoot that would grow from the stump of Jesse (Isa. 11:1–10; cf. Jer. 33:15) would become a majestic cedar providing peace for all who dwell in its branches (Ezek. 17:23).[8] Christ Himself, the Seed of the kingdom (Gal. 3:16), seems small and insignificant in the world's eyes. But one day every knee will bow before Him (Rom. 14:11). John Calvin—a man familiar with discouragement—writes of this parable, "Let us not despond, but rise by faith against the pride of the world, till the Lord give us that astonishing display of his power, of which he speaks in this passage."[9]

### A Final Warning: Take Heed! (4:21–25)

The Bible describes unbelievers as stopping their ears so that they can barely hear the Word of God (Acts 7:57). Those who suppress God's revelation do so to their own destruction. Still, despite the best of human earplugs, God's Word still trickles in. For this reason, none of us should forget Jesus' words about the responsibility that comes with receiving divine revelation. As the light of the world, Jesus will make Himself known at some point to every person who has ever lived. When we hear, we must take heed; we will be held accountable for what we hear. For believers, this warning comes with an invitation to make known what we know (Matt. 10:27) and to shine as lights in the world in the midst of a crooked and perverse generation (Phil 2:15; cf. Matt. 5:14–16).

## Questions

1. From which Old Testament texts is Mark 4:12 drawn? How do the context of those texts shed light on Jesus' message?
2. Spend some time reflecting on the similarities and differences between farming in your context and farming in Jesus' context, and how these thoughts affect our understanding of Mark 4.
3. What does it mean to "have no root in themselves" (Mark 4:17)?
4. How can "the cares of this world" choke out the gospel (Mark 4:19)?
5. How can riches be deceitful (Mark 4:19)? Can you share a few ways in which you have learned to hear and accept the word (Mark 4:20)?
6. Are there ways in which you or your group are like a lamp under a basket (Mark 4:21)?
7. How have you witnessed the truth of Mark 4:26–28?
8. How does the book of Acts begin to fulfill Jesus' words in Mark 4:30–32?

1. Accessed on September 15, 2009 from http://www.leftlanenews.com/bob-like-a-rock-seger-no-chevy-driver.html.

2. *Canons of Dort,* 1.6.

3. Herman Hanko, *The Mysteries of the Kingdom: An Exposition of the Parables* (Grand Rapids: Reformed Free Publishing Association, 1975), 14.

4. In fact, "in treating the word of God so lightly they are co-operating with the prince of evil!" (v. 15). William Hendriksen, *Exposition of the Gospel According to Mark*, New Testament Commentary (Grand Rapids: Baker, 1976), 156.

5. *Ibid.*, 158.

6. For an expanded treatment of these themes see William Boekestein, "Profiting from Preaching: Learning to Truly Hear God," *The Outlook* 64:4 (2014): 22–24.

7. Hendriksen, *Mark*, 165.

8. Jesus may also be alluding to the positive influence of the kingdom on society. The reference to the birds of the air suggests that the kingdom provides blessing even to the unbelieving world. Note how "birds of the air" is used in a previous parable (Mark 4:1, 15) as a symbol of the unbelieving world; in fact of Satan himself.

9. John Calvin, *Harmony of the Gospels* (Grand Rapids: Baker, 1989), vol. 2, 127.

# CHRIST CONQUERS FOES

**Mark 4:35–5:43**

In each of the stories in our text Jesus responds to a problem. This problem-response motif tells us something about ourselves and about Jesus.

It tells us that after our fall into sin, "man is born to trouble as the sparks fly upward" (Job 5:7). Man's manifold problems can be traced back to Genesis 3:6. There were no life-threatening storms in paradise. There were no dangerous, demon-possessed men in the Garden of Eden. There was neither illness nor human death before sin entered the world. In this text we catch a glimpse of life in paradise lost, the same world through which we walk today.

But the theme of our text also tells us that Christ is the great restorer. Christ calms the storm, sets captives free, heals the sick, and raises the dead. Christ is God's answer to the problems caused by sin. That's good news for people surrounded by pervasive defect. We are broken people; more so than we sometimes realize. As Adam's heirs deformity seems so natural to us. We need to be restored by the second Adam (1 Cor. 15:45).

In this passage Mark shows Jesus' authority over four post-fall defects that tend to cause so much anxiety in the hearts of the sons of Adam: disaster, demons, disease, and death.

## Christ's Power over Disaster (4:35–41)

Jesus had spent an exhausting day telling a host of parables about the kingdom of God (4:33–34). And though evening had come, His work was not over. He alone knew that a demonized man living across the Sea of Galilee needed new life. So He said to His disciples, "Let us cross over to the other side" (4:35).

As the disciples navigated the Sea of Galilee a great storm arose. Waves crashed over the boat, tossing it about, filling it with water. Even the seasoned seamen had that sick feeling you might get after a carnival ride. In their panic the disciples staggered to the back of the ship only to find Jesus . . . sleeping. Our son is a virtuosic sleeper who can slumber through almost any condition. He once fell asleep slumped over an ottoman in a loud, crowded room. When we picked him up we found that he was resting on top of a pile of toys. (Maybe you know someone like him!) But I doubt even he could have slept through this storm. Yet, Jesus slept.

In despair, the disciples interpreted Jesus' sleep as a sign of His disinterest in their well-being: "He doesn't care that we are perishing" (v. 38). But the disciples' allegation was exactly wrong. Jesus slept through the storm because He was exhausted from working on behalf of His people. As Calvin says, Christ saves us by His entire obedience, not just His obedience on the cross but the obedience of His entire life.[1] Jesus' obedience was physically draining. Still the disciples' insulting comment had some truth to it. From a human perspective they were perishing. Matthew says the boat was "being swamped by the waves" (Matt. 8:24, RSV). Luke adds that the disciples were "in great danger" (Luke 8:23, NIV). These skilled fishermen knew rough waters; they were afraid for good reason. If their ship sank they would die. But Jesus made it clear that the deeper problem was their lack of trust in God. "How is it that you have no faith?" (v. 40). The main problem was not the storm but the inability of their faith to withstand the storm. And yet, when we coalesce the disciples' responses as recorded in the three Synoptic Gospels, we see that in their weakness of faith, they rightly reached out to Christ as their only hope: "We are perishing. Do you care? Save, Lord!"[2] In reply, Jesus chastened them for their weak faith, but He did not condemn them. Instead, He saved. We too can call on the Lord in our trouble anticipating His response: "Peace, be still."

Mark says that Jesus rebuked the wind. We don't realize how radical this is until we think about how little power our words have to change a situation. Have you ever heard a mother tell her children to "stop it," as if she were a broken record . . . and nothing happened? Imagine standing outside during the next thunderstorm and telling the rain, wind, and lightning to "be still!" This is what Jesus did. His words instantly shackled the wind and slapped the waves still.

How amazing; though Christ's authority extends over every atom of the universe, He willingly submitted to the agonies of the cross. In the garden of Gethsemane He could have commanded the olive trees to fall on Judas before he betrayed Him. He could have directed the ground to swallow the advancing company of soldiers. Standing before Pilate He could have spoken one word and caused that cowardly governor to choke on his own tongue rather than give consent to crucify Him. Although Christ has the entire universe at His disposal, He willingly laid down His life for us.

## Christ's Power over Demons (5:1–20)

Upon landing on the other side of the Galilean sea, in the country of the Gentiles, Jesus and His disciples met a man who was possessed by an unclean spirit. As I write, images of demons, tombs, and chains are springing up in front of homes and stores in anticipation of Halloween. The irony is that people today celebrate the very things that characterized this man's miserable life. Not only was this man's life a wreck, but also he was so "fierce . . . that no one could pass that way" (Matt. 8:28). He was like that angry dog in the yard that would keep you from even thinking about walking through the front gate. But there was a deeper problem. This man—and his countrymen—were lost, having no saving knowledge of God. Jesus was in the land of the Gentiles, who had "no hope and [who were] without God in the world" (Eph. 2:12).

Again, Jesus healed with a spoken word. Matthew records Jesus saying one word to the demons: "Go!" The result was similar to the previous story. The man ceased his raging, regained his right mind, and stopped endangering his neighbors. Even more than that, because of his testimony, many were brought to Christ.

This passage teaches us that the forces of evil answer to Jesus (cf. Job 1:6–12). "He gave them permission" to leave the man (Mark 5:13). The demons even recognized Jesus as their Lord by calling Him the Son of the Most High God (5:7). Believers can say with David, "Yea, though I walk through the valley of the shadow of death, I will fear no evil; for You are with me" (Ps. 23:4). Having God with us in the midst of evil would be no great comfort if He wasn't also in charge of that evil. Cancers, bullies, politicians, and atmospheric carbon all answer to King Jesus. The believer is assured that "whatever evil [God] sends upon me in this vale of tears, He will turn to my good."[3]

We also learn that salvation is a sovereign act of God. Like the thief on the cross, this man contributed nothing to his deliverance. Unflattering as it is, this man is a reflection of every person whom Jesus delivers from sin's powerful chains. With one word, Jesus frees condemned sinners from the chains of bondage. We can't contribute to our salvation, but we can cry out to God confessing our misery, asking for freedom, being confident that He will hear us.

Finally, this healing enforces a mandate to personal evangelism. Notably, Jesus commanded the former demoniac to begin witnessing to those with whom he had a built-in connection. In witnessing, our own families and friends must claim our first attention. And as we hear Jesus' call to explain our hope (1 Peter 3:15) we should be careful not to complicate our calling. Personal witnessing is much simpler than we sometimes make it. It doesn't require a seminary education; indeed, Jesus forbade this man from joining His "seminary." Personal witnessing is as simple as telling our friends what great things the Lord has done for us and how He has had compassion on us (5:19). In Jesus' estimation prompt obedience, even by those with little knowledge, is greatly valued. Those who tell what they can about their reception of grace can anticipate still greater evangelistic opportunities (Luke 16:10), while those who wait to witness until they have accumulated greater theological wherewithal might very well never begin to witness. The devil's favorite word is "later."

## Jesus' Power over Disease and Death (5:21–43)

As Jesus returned from the land of the Gentiles He was greeted by a multitude of Galileans who likewise needed restoration. From the midst of the crowd a man named Jairus pushed his way to Christ with an earnest request.

### An Earnest Request (5:21–24)

Jairus's request is an example of simple, humble, and confident prayer. After explaining the problem in a few words he simply asked Jesus, "Come and lay Your hands on [my daughter]," who "lies at the point of death." Jairus shows us that true prayer doesn't require flashy, elaborate language. Jairus's request is also humble. Being a synagogue ruler Jairus was either a Pharisee or a Sadducee. However condescending, arrogant, and self-righteous he might have been before, personal neediness brought him to Jesus' feet. Such humility, though, should not conflict with confidence. "If you lay your hands on her she will be healed," he said (v. 23). Like the leper of Mark 1:40, the four friends of Mark 2:4–5, and the ailing woman of Mark 5:28, Jairus approached the fount of healing with boldness on behalf of his unconscious daughter. These examples teach us to "come boldly to the throne of grace, that we may obtain mercy and find grace to help in time of need" (Heb. 4:16).

*An Encouraging Interruption (5:25–35)*
Right as Jesus began to follow Jairus home He was interrupted by a woman who had been bleeding for a dozen years. Imagine how Jairus must have felt. His daughter was at the point of death, and Jesus was stopping to interact with a woman who had been coping with her issue for as long as his daughter has been alive! How would you feel if your child were trapped in a burning house, and as a first responder was about to enter one of your neighbors walked up and said to him, "Sir, I've got this chronic back pain that I just can't seem to shake. Could you take a look?" But Jesus allowed Himself to be interrupted for the same reason He would later hesitate in the situation with Lazarus (John 11:15). God sometimes allows situations to worsen in order to draw us closer and to reveal His glory to those who are faithful during trials. Jesus also stopped for the sake of the woman. His question, "Who touched me?" wasn't asked in ignorance. He wanted to prove to the woman that He healed her because of His willingness to graciously reward her faith, not because His clothes were magical.

While Jesus was pronouncing healing upon the woman, a man from Jairus's house delivered a crushing blow to his master: "Your daughter is dead. Why bother the Teacher any further?" (v. 35). His only daughter, the one who had been the object of his affection and the joy of his home, was gone

(Luke 8:42). Right when he was daring to hope, his servant— in a spirit of unbelief—dashed his hope to the ground. In the servant's eyes, Jesus might have been able to help a sick girl but not a dead girl. Unbelief imagines one's problems as towering over a puny God. Faith confesses the absolute superiority of God over every problem.

*A Joyful Resolution (5:36–43)*

Jesus used the occasion of the death of Jairus's daughter to minister to three groups of people. First, Jesus commanded Jairus not to be afraid but to believe. Only Luke records Jesus promise: "believe, and she will be made well" (8:50). We don't always have the luxury of knowing that our faith will be so immediately rewarded. Still, God calls us to believe. The good news, says Jesus, is that God is worth holding onto even when everything that comes through His hands seems to be against us. A time is coming in your life when the bottom will seem to fall out. "Don't be afraid, only believe." Believe that He who takes away is the one who gave in the first place. Believe that He who allows hurt is also the one who heals. Believe that God uses pain and trial and loss to steer the Christian toward heaven.

Second, Jesus interacted with the mourners. He asked them an unusual question: "Why make this commotion and weep? The child is not dead, but sleeping" (5:39). The crowd found this laughable (v. 40); they had seen the dead body, some may have touched the cool skin. They laughed, not understanding what Jesus would later tell His friend Martha: "I am the resurrection and the life. He who believes in Me, though he may die, he shall live" (John 11:25).

Finally, in one of the most precious scenes in the entire Bible, which no mocker was permitted to witness (5:40), Jesus woke the "sleeping" little girl. You can imagine the parents breaking into tears again as Jesus tenderly led them into the room in which the lifeless corpse of their precious daughter lay. In amazement they watched Jesus take their daughter's hand and say to her, "Little girl, I say to you, arise" (5:41). At that word, her brain began sending signals again, her heart began pumping, the color returned to her skin, and she began breathing. Soon she opened her eyes, sat up, starting walking, and even had a meal. Restoration!

Ultimately these narratives look to a day when all things will be completely restored (Acts 3:21). The waves of Galilee raged again, Jairus's daughter eventually died again, the woman with the issue of blood eventually had other bodily problems before she too died. But this narrative looks ahead to a greater restoration. Don't miss that when Jesus took the little girl's hand He did something radical. We might not notice (though Jairus, the synagogue leader, would have) that Jesus intentionally became ceremonially unclean (Num. 19:13). Galatians 3:13 explains why: "Christ has redeemed us from the curse of the law, having become a curse for us." Jesus works restoration by taking our uncleanness upon Himself and exchanging our sin for His glorious righteousness.

Where do you need restoration? J. C. Ryle reminds us, commenting on this passage, that "with the Lord Jesus Christ nothing is impossible. No stormy passions are so strong but that he can tame them. No temper is so rough and violent but that he can change it. No conscience so [bothered], but he can speak peace to it, and make it calm. No man ever need despair, if he will only bow down his pride, and come as a humbled sinner to Christ."[4]

## Questions

1. Does the fact that Jesus slept while the disciples fretted trouble or encourage you?

2. How does Colossians 1:16–17 help answer the question asked in Mark 4:41?

3. Reflect on the contrast between man's ineptitude (in Mark 5:4) and Jesus' power (in Mark 5:13–15).

4. How should Mark 5:8 encourage those who battle against "spiritual hosts of wickedness" (Eph. 6:12)?

5. Can those without "Damascus road conversions" (Acts 9) still tell their friends what great things the Lord has done for them?

6. Spend some time identifying and praying for your friends to whom you are called to witness Christ's redemption (see Mark 5:19).

7. What does the phrase "one of the rulers of the synagogue" add to the narrative of the healing of Jairus's daughter?

8. Why does Jesus ask the strange question recorded in Mark 5:30–31?

9. In what way does faith cast out fear (see Mark 5:36)?

1. John Calvin, *Institutes of the Christian Religion* (Grand Rapids: Eerdmans, 1962), 2.16.5.

2. Matthew 8:25; Mark 4:38; Luke 8:24.

3. *Heidelberg Catechism*, Q&A 26.

4. J. C. Ryle, *Expository Thoughts on the Gospels: Mark* (New York: Robert Carter & Brothers, 1866), 85.

# THE KINGDOM HONORED AND DISHONORED

▶ ● ◀

## Mark 6:1–29

How do you deal with rejection? In our fallen world that's an important question. One of the major themes in Mark 6:1–29 is that those who live and die in the joy of heavenly comfort still face huge disappointments. In this passage the church's cornerstone and the most significant men of the apostolic church all deal with rejection. This great cloud of witnesses urges us to run with endurance the challenging race that is set before us (Heb. 12:1). As we learned in Mark 4, one of the purposes of the four Gospels is to show how the kingdom starts small, gains momentum despite setbacks, and eventually changes the lives of millions.

There are three distinct rejection narratives in Mark 6:1–29. In the first we see the rejection of our Lord.

### Marvelous Unbelief (6:1–6)

In the previous narrative Jesus did what you might expect God to do. He conquered nature, subdued demons, disarmed disease, and defeated death. In the last passage Jesus raised to life the daughter of a synagogue ruler. When Jesus came to the synagogue in Nazareth (6:2) we might expect Him to have received a hero's welcome. Amazingly people stumbled over Him, questioning Jesus' background and authority. Even Jesus "marveled because of their unbelief" (6:6). Remarkable as it is, the Bible teaches that people will always be offended at Jesus until their eyes and ears are opened and their hearts are made soft toward Him (Ps. 119:18). The more we understand this truth the more resistant we will be to sugar-coat the gospel to make it more appealing. The Bible says that all men are sinners and guilty of the eternal punishment of hell. God alone removes our guilt by forgiving our sins for the sake of Christ's life, death, and resurrection. That is an inherently offensive message! Only the Holy Spirit can make us embrace the gospel as He mollifies our resistance to the things of God (John 3:5–8).

The Third Evangelist provides some important details explaining the specific points at which the crowds stumbled over Jesus (Luke 4:16–30). Jesus' preaching text was from Isaiah 61, where God promises a spirit-anointed gospel minister who would come to heal the brokenhearted, set captives free, give sight to the blind, and proclaim the acceptable year of the Lord. From the perspective of the audience, the problem came when, after handing the scroll back to the attendant and waiting until every eye was fixed on Him, Jesus said, "Today this Scripture is fulfilled in your hearing" (Luke 4:21). The crowd wondered how this man was qualified to make such a statement. Ironically, God answered the question at the beginning of Jesus' ministry, specifically at His baptism. When God anointed Him with the Holy Spirit He commissioned Him to mediate for God's people as their perfect prophet, priest, and king. He audibly declared, "You are My beloved Son, in whom I am well pleased" (Mark 1:11). Jesus received His authority from His heavenly Father. Christ came to the Jews, as He comes to all people, with a divine right to our allegiance.

The authority of Christ is incredibly encouraging for those who submit to it. Believers communicate the gospel to others with divine authority (Matt. 28:18–20). How much it should mean to us to have the risen, reigning, and returning Christ standing behind us when we witness to His glory! Sometimes my son tries, on his own authority, to get his little sister do something. His efforts sound timid to say the least: "Eva, let's go in the house, c'mon Eva, it's time to go in . . ." But sometimes I send him to get her on my authority. You should hear the change in his tone of voice: "EVA, DAD SAID, 'COME IN THE HOUSE!'" Our witness will be transformed as we increasingly glory in the authority of Christ.

The crowd also questioned Jesus' background. "Is this not the carpenter?" (v. 3). The word used by the crowd can be translated as "craftsman." Though they perhaps spoke derisively (he's the tinkerer), they also spoke prophetically. Jesus is the master craftsman of the kingdom of God (Heb. 3:1–6; 11:10) and of all creation (Col. 3:16), yet He humbled Himself by coming to the earth and taking up a common trade. To the believer Christ's vocation as a carpenter is a wonderful condescension. To the unbeliever it is one more occasion to doubt and mock. Similarly, the doubters scoffed at Jesus' family tree because they failed to grasp the incarnation. They saw Jesus as the son of Mary, the brother of James, Joses, Judas, and Simon. They didn't see him as the Son of God who transcends genealogy to meet sinners from every family of the earth.

In response to this rejection, Jesus reminded the people of a sad trend in Israel's history: Prophets are always dishonored at home. In another setting Jesus said to the Pharisees, "Woe to you! For you build the tombs of the prophets, and your fathers killed them" (Luke 11:47). In a similar way Stephen would say, "Which of the prophets did your fathers not persecute? And they killed those who foretold the coming of the Just One, of whom you now have become the betrayers and murderers" (Acts 7:52). Jesus came to His own knowing that His own would not receive Him (John 1:11). Amazingly, He persevered in His ministry going about the "villages in a circuit, teaching" (Mark 6:6) although, because of their unbelief, Jesus did shroud His power among them, doing fewer miracles there than elsewhere (v. 5).

Is it a coincidence that Jesus began to deploy His disciples just as the crowds voiced their skepticism over His ministry?

## The Apostolic Ministry (6:7–13)

Jesus' sending of the disciples into the mission field depicts the Gospels' powerful movement in the face of rejection. In some ways this is the first Great Commission. The disciples have been trained and empowered; now they are commissioned. Part of their commissioning service was meant to strip them of material comforts (6:8–9). Disciples—especially those who live in a context of rampant materialism—must not find security in material possessions but in the good providence of God which believers experience through the care of brothers and sisters. The church should reflect this pattern of healthy interdependency among believers and ultimate dependency on God.

The disciples' light load—Jesus "commanded them to take nothing for the journey except a staff" (6:8)—would not only require them to depend on the care of "worthy" saints (Matt. 10:11–13) but also allow them to be highly mobile. It would be clear to the disciples whether or not their listeners were receiving the message. Those who refused to listen, that is, "all unbelievers and such as do not sincerely repent," needed to hear that "the wrath of God and eternal condemnation abide on them so long as they are not converted."[1] "It will be more tolerable for Sodom and Gomorrah" than for those who reject the gospel ministry (Mark 6:11); this fact should send shivers down our spines and drive us to feel the necessity of believing the gospel for ourselves and of imploring others to believe it too. Jesus' instructions to His first evangelists mandates the church today to continuously refocus its evangelistic efforts toward those who are have not rejected the gospel. Like the disciples, we need to be aware that God both shuts and opens doors (Acts 16:6–10), and we must exert our finite energies accordingly.

Mark's encouraging report on the success of the disciples' first tour (Mark 6:12–13) highlights three ministry components which the church that is built on their foundation (Eph. 2:20) must emulate. First, Mark says that they "preached that people should repent." True ministry always uses the law to reveal man's radical failures (Rom. 3:20).[2] When the Spirit moves us to see our miserable condition before the law we cry out with Paul, "O wretched man that I am! Who will deliver me from this body of death? I thank God—through Jesus Christ our Lord!" (Rom. 7:24–25). In this way the law serves as "our schoolmaster to bring us unto Christ, that we might be justified by faith" (Gal. 3:24). Every so often I'm asked if our church has altar calls. We certainly do. We don't ask folks to come forward to a physical altar, but we do believe that every sermon should call sinners to repent and believe the gospel. We should "always teach that an entrance unto God is open for all sinners, and that this God does forgive all the sins of the faithful."[3]

Second, the disciples dealt with devils. Somehow, what is central to the first apostles' mandate tends to get minimized in some Christian traditions. We need to believe that the same demonic powers which are so evident in the Scripture story have not relented. Neither has the means of fighting demons changed; it remains the gospel ministry. Paul warned believers to arm themselves with God's armor to "stand against the wiles of the devil" and to wrestle "against principalities, against powers, against the rulers of the darkness of this age, against spiritual hosts of wickedness in the heavenly places" (Eph. 6:11–12). There is a side to gospel ministry that is darker than many churchgoers might be interested in. When churches really begin to imitate the apostles, they find themselves dealing with the occult, with drug addicts, pedophiles, fornicators, homosexual offenders, pornographers, and the like (cf. 1 Cor. 6:9–11). Like the disciples, churches and individuals who truly wrestle against Satan's kingdom find that Christian ministry is not safe and sanitary. But, like the disciples, they find that Christ is still casting out demons and beating back the kingdom of Satan.

Finally, the disciples were concerned with the ill and hurting (Mark 6:13). The apostle John would later write about what he learned on that first ministry circuit: "But whoever has this world's goods, and sees his brother in need, and shuts up his heart from him, how does the love of God abide in him? My little children, let us not love in word or in tongue, but in deed and in truth" (1 John 3:17–18). The social gospel is faulty not because of its emphasis on humanitarian work but because its humanitarian work is not vitally connected to the true gospel of the work of Christ in securing the salvation of His people.

In these first two narratives of Mark 6 Jesus and His disciples are both honored and dishonored as they engage in ministry. The final narrative in this section describes the honor and dishonor shown to John the Baptist.

## A Christian Martyr (6:14–29)

Mark 6:14 tells us that the commotion surrounding Jesus eventually reached the ears of King Herod, who thought Jesus was John the Baptist raised from the dead. Mark then explains what had happened to John the Baptist, an important excursus because John hasn't been mentioned since Mark 1:14. It was after John's imprisonment that Jesus began His public ministry. From that point John faded from the Gospel writer's attention, something that he would have been glad about (John 3:30).

John was imprisoned for the stance he took against King Herod's marriage to Herod's sister-in-law, Herodias. As a result Herodias "held it against him and wanted to kill John" (Mark 6:19). Herodias's response illustrates what happens when preaching hits close to home, as it must. It's one thing to say, "Repent." It's another thing to say, "Repent for committing adultery" (v. 18). John used the law like a sharp scalpel in the hands of a skilled surgeon. He targeted a specific sin which revealed the couple's sin-sick hearts. Too often our counsel to sinners more closely resembles personal advice than legal reproof. Had we been in John's shoes we might have offered statistics demonstrating that adultery adversely affects one's happiness. Instead, John honestly revealed the bad news while urging them to use the remedy of repentance. Herodias responded with the well-worn saw, "Don't judge me!" Sadly, such an attitude leads to a judgment worse than that which befell Sodom and Gomorrah (v. 11).

Herod, too, failed to deal with his sin by repentance. The king was exceedingly sorry for murdering John—but he did it anyway! Godly sorrow would have led the king to repent by breaking his wicked oath regardless of the influence of those who sat with him (v. 26a). How often do we pretend to grieve over what we are doing but continue to do it? Repentance is a change of mind that brings about a change of action. Repentance is not merely to say "I'm sorry" (something we might say if we sneeze in someone else's direction). Repentance is saying, "I've been wrong, but now I see the truth and am willing to be transformed by it." Sorrow not leading to repentance is a sham which needs to be repented of (2 Cor. 7:9–10).

John the Baptist and the apostles were rejected for unmistakably siding with God. They followed Christ as ambassadors who represented the kingdom of God in opposition to the kingdom of this world. Therefore, they spoke on behalf of God against sin—and were soundly opposed. I don't want to be opposed. I want to fit in. I am tempted to shrink back when I hear that "all who desire to live godly in Christ Jesus will suffer persecution" (2 Tim. 3:12). But in opposition we find hope.

The ultimate hope for those who are rejected by the world is found the return of Christ. In fact, Mark hints, ever so slightly, at the significance of the return of Christ in what the disciples did with the severed head and body of John the Baptist: they laid them in a tomb (Mark 6:29). They had regard for John's dismembered body because they knew that his body would be raised up and remade into a glorious body. No amount of rejection is worthy of comparison with the glory which will be revealed in us when Christ returns (Rom. 8:18). If we pay too little attention to Christ's return it might be because we become so comfortable in this present age.

John Calvin was a man familiar with rejection but who found his hope in the return of Christ and the resurrection of the body. He ended nearly every one of his theological lectures with a short prayer, most of which concluded with a reference to our glorious inheritance which Christ will one day deliver to us. With Calvin we pray:

> Grant, Almighty God, since you do not cease your daily exhortations to repentance, but do indulge us, and bear with us, while you correct us by your word and your chastisements, that we may not remain obstinate, but may learn to submit ourselves to you: Grant, [we] pray, that we may not offer ourselves as your disciples with feigned repentance, but be so sincerely and cordially devoted to you, that we may desire nothing else than to progress more and more in the knowledge of your heavenly doctrine, till at length we enjoy that full light which we hope for through our Lord Jesus Christ. Amen.[4]

## Questions

1. Why are prophets exceptionally dishonored in their own home (Mark 6:6)? Are there any ways in which we experience this truth?

2. How can churches today actively bring the gospel from house to house as the first disciples did (Mark 6:10)?

3. Why does Jesus promise greater punishment for those who rejected the apostles than for Sodom and Gomorrah?

4. How does Mark 6:12–13 help shape the gospel ministry today?

5. How is Mark 6:14–29 an elaboration on Mark 6:12?

6. What do we learn about Herod's character from our text?

7. What do we learn about John the Baptist's character from our text?

8. In Mark 6:29, do the disciples teach us anything about caring for the bodies of the deceased?

9. Our text describes both setbacks and victories. In what way is the overall tone of the chapter positive?

1. *Heidelberg Catechism*, Q&A 84.
2. Cf. *Heidelberg Catechism*, Q&A 2: "Whence do you know your misery? Out of the law of God."
3. *Second Helvetic Confession*, 14.8.
4. From Calvin's sixty-third lecture on Ezekiel. John Calvin, *Commentaries on the First Twenty Chapters of the Book of the Prophet Ezekiel* (Grand Rapids: Baker Book House, 1989), 325.

# MINISTRY AROUND THE SEA OF GALILEE

————————————➤ ● ◄————————————

**Mark 6:30–56**

The Bible warns against eating the food of a stingy man. "He is the kind of man who is always thinking about the cost. 'Eat and drink,' he says to you, but his heart is not with you" (Prov. 23:6–7). Sadly, many people view God as such a stingy man. They doubt that God wants them to be happy. They fear that He allows them to receive blessings only to snatch them just as quickly from their hands. They insist that God is tight-fisted with His gifts.

The second half of Mark 6 destroys any such notion of God.

Despite being shamefully treated by those He came to bless (Mark 6:4) Jesus continued to represent His heavenly Father by laboring generously in the midst of those who dishonored Him.[1] Despite their unbelief, Jesus tenderly ministered to His disciples. He was moved with compassion for vast crowds of people, even though they misunderstand His mission (John 6:15). Christ's open hands and heart reveal God as the "overflowing fountain of all good."[2]

## Jesus Feeds the Five Thousand (6:30–44)

*The Disciples Report Back (6:30–32)*

The disciples' excitement was palpable. They had just returned from their first tour of preaching and teaching. No doubt they had experienced both encouragement and disappointment. They had probably exhibited bravery and hesitation. But like generals reporting to their commander-in-chief they told Jesus everything that had happened (6:30). Like these first disciples, modern-day disciples need not keep anything from Jesus. Sometimes in our prayers we pick and choose the things we want to say to the Lord. Sometimes we are reluctant to become too transparent. How often do we forget that "God [will] search this out for He knows the secrets of the heart" (Ps. 44:21)?

The disciples also remind us of the importance of spiritual conversation. How often do we talk about what God is doing in our lives? What distinguishes our conversations from those of unbelievers should be more than the omission of vulgarity. God is at work in the lives of His children. Whether He is leading us through spiritual deserts or gardens we have something to talk about. Spiritual conversations are not opportunities for us to boast about our work. They are opportunities to point out God's persistent grace in our weaknesses and struggles. Talking about what God is doing in our lives is one way that we can "consider one another in order to stir up love and good works" (Heb. 10:24).

With their adrenaline running high after returning from the battlefield, and the bustle of the crowds that had begun to gather around, the itinerant preachers might not have noticed their need to rest and eat. But Jesus did. "Come aside by yourselves to a deserted place and rest a while," He said (6:31). Spiritual activity, as important as it is, doesn't cancel our need to care for our bodies. Jesus teaches us that it is a spiritual discipline to eat and rest. There was an old heresy called Gnosticism which taught the separation of matter and spirit. Because matter was essentially evil (and spirit essentially good) what happens in the body is of no importance. Christianity, it was said, is spiritual not physical. It has been convincingly argued that a neo-Gnostic neglect of the body is pervasive among Christians today. By contrast, "a renewed understanding of our full-orbed creatureliness, with due place given to the body, will produce safety, piety, productivity, and creativity."[3] We glorify God in our bodies, which are the temples of the Holy Spirit (1 Cor. 6:19–20), by scheduling times of rest and relaxation and learning to say no to unnecessarily wearying demands.

Thus instructed, tired and hungry disciples headed to one of the most deserted places they could imagine: a boat on the open water. They intended to cross over to the other side of the Sea of Galilee to a city called Bethsaida (cf. John 6:1; Luke 9:10). But like modern paparazzi the enthralled crowd "ran there on foot from all the cities. They arrived before them and came together to Him" (6:33).

### Jesus Teaches the Crowds (6:33–34)

Jesus and His disciples sought rest but found a crowd. Can you imagine how you might have responded in their situation? Sometimes we just want to "turn off" for a while. We don't want to be called. We don't want to be busy. We want to recuperate. This is just what Jesus sought for Himself and His friends. And, as mentioned, sometimes this is necessary. Yet, when He saw the crowd He was "moved with compassion for them" (6:34) and "welcomed them and spoke to them about the kingdom of God and cured those who had need of healing" (Luke 9:11, NIV).

What was it that moved Jesus to set aside His own physical and mental well-being for the crowds? He saw them as sheep without a shepherd. The Jewish religious leaders were not leading the people to the green pastures of God's grace. Instead they—not unlike some ministers today—emphasized a system of religious duties. As the good shepherd Christ's heart went out to these lost sheep. Moved with compassion, He began to teach the gospel. The gospel is still a window into Jesus' compassionate heart. It tells us that God knows our weaknesses and our sins, yet He takes pleasure in saving sinners (Ezek. 33:11).

*The Miraculous Feeding (6:35–44)*

As the crowd listened to Jesus the disciples grew increasingly uncomfortable. How were they going to feed the countless thousands who had gathered (Matt. 14:21)? Showing a truly miserly spirit the disciples wanted to send the people away for food. "After all," they thought, "we didn't ask them to come here. We certainly don't have to feed them." How often do we take that same approach to "outsiders"? Jesus did not consider it extravagant to care for the physical needs of the crowds even though many of them were there only to be entertained. Even though they would eventually demand His crucifixion, He fed them. Rather than seeing the crowds as a problem, Jesus saw them as an opportunity to showcase God's superabundant provision. God's people need to learn from Jesus to do the same.

Jesus also fed the crowd to test the faith of the disciples (cf. John 6:6): they acknowledged it would cost 200 denarii— more than half a year's wages—to feed everyone present (Mark 6:37). What was Jesus calling them to do? The disciples were still learning that Christ's call to discipleship stretches His followers beyond their natural abilities, demanding us to depend on Him. The disciples despaired when they calculated the cost. Christ was teaching them to count the cost, realize that it is more than they can pay, and turn to Him for help. The fact that Jesus would shortly repeat this miracle of a great feeding (Mark 8:1–10) shows us His commitment to open closed eyes and soften hard hearts (8:18).

After the magnanimous feeding, Jesus immediately dispersed the crowd, perceiving that they were about to forcibly make Him a king, and escaped to the mountain alone to pray (John 6:15). Jesus was, as the crowds suspected, "truly the Prophet who is to come into the world" (John 6:14), but this was neither the time nor the manner in which He would reveal His glory. Jesus sent His disciples on ahead by boat to meet Him in Bethsaida while he retreated to the mountain to pray.[4]

## Jesus Walks on Water (6:45–52)

*Jesus Alone (6:45–47)*

Mark doesn't tell us what Jesus was praying about on the mountain. But, considering that Jesus could see His disciples "straining at rowing" against difficult winds, we have every reason to believe that He was praying for His disciples' apparently futile struggle. Jesus was preparing His students for another lesson. He had made them get into the boat and go to the other side (6:45). Then, being God, He caused the great wind to prevail against them (6:48). John says, "The sea arose because a great wind was blowing" (John 6:18). Matthew says that "the boat was now in the middle of the sea, tossed by the waves, for the wind was contrary" (Matt. 14:24). But the whole time, Jesus was watching them in intercessory prayer!

Couldn't Christ's intercession change the way we look at life's challenges? Children of God can have confidence that Christ is watching them from the throne of heaven as they battle against a barrage of temptations.[5] In His loving providence God leads His children into trying circumstances even as Jesus was "led by the spirit into the wilderness, being tempted for forty days by the devil" (Luke 4:1–2). At the same time, "the Lord knows how to deliver the godly out of temptations" (2 Peter 2:9). With that knowledge Christ always prays (Heb. 7:25) for His children to resist sin, and that their "faith should not fail" (Luke 22:31). Whether God's children wrestle with sexual sins, difficult doctor's appointments, or disobedient children, Christ is praying for them.

*A Miraculous Walk (6:48)*

Again, Jesus is moved by compassion for His hurting children. He waited long enough for the disciples to realize that they strained against the wind in vain. Then, "He came to them, walking on the sea, and would have passed them by" (6:48). That sounds strange, doesn't it? Why would Jesus walk by His disciples in their moment of need? Scripture doesn't answer. But, remember, Jesus had no need to walk to the boat; He was doing just fine walking on the water! He walked near the boat to encourage the disciples with His presence. He could well have walked past the boat guiding it to the shore through the storm.

### The Disciples Are Amazed (6:49–52)

You might think that the sight of their Savior walking toward them would fill the disciples with hope. Instead, they "cried out . . . and were troubled" (6:49–50). In order to understand why the disciples responded with fear we need to know two things about them. First, they were superstitious; they had an irrational fear of the unknown. Granted, it's very unusual to see the shape of a man walking on the water, but why should the disciples assume the worst? Why did they not rather assume that it was an angel of God, if not Christ Himself? Given the natural tendency to superstition that we share with the disciples, we should refuse to engage the dark spiritual realm for the sake of entertainment. Horror movies and other dark arts cater to the same sort of superstitious fear with which the disciples seemed to be filled. With Martin Luther, we must face the devil-filled-world with the perspective of a warrior, not a spectator.

> And though this world with devils filled should threaten to undo us,
>
> We will not fear, for God has willed His truth to triumph through us.
>
> The prince of darkness grim, we tremble not for him;
>
> His rage we can endure, for lo, his doom is sure; one little word shall fell him.

Second, the disciples responded to Jesus' presence with fear because their hearts were hardened (6:52). Even after

Jesus urged them not to be afraid, and after He had calmed the wind, "they were greatly amazed in themselves beyond measure, and marveled" (6:51). Mark adds this comment: "For they had not understood about the loaves because their heart was hardened" (6:52). The disciples' hard hearts prevented them from grasping the significance of the loaves. What does this mean? They failed to understand that in union with Christ we lack nothing. Earlier they were concerned about their lack of food. Now they were terrified about their lack of security. They had not yet learned that Jesus meets every need of His children. Nonetheless, as William Hendriksen points out, the hardness of the disciples' hearts needs to be distinguished from the hard-heartedness of the unbelieving scribes and Pharisees.[6] Believers can have hard hearts owing to lapses in faith. In this connection, Matthew includes Peter's failed attempt to walk on water to illustrate that not only Peter, but all disciples, are at times people of little faith, prone to doubt (Matt. 14:31). Unbelievers' hard hearts are not owing to a temporary lapse in faith but to the obstinacy and hatred with which they reject Christ.

With God's help, the disciples reached the other shore, setting anchor in the land of Gennesaret—a region south of Capernaum. By such deliverance the Lord graciously continued to soften their hard hearts.

## Jesus Heals the Masses (6:53–56)

What happened next should no longer surprise us. Immediately upon landing people recognized Jesus and began to spread the news. An ambulance industry had cropped up around Jesus. Men would run through the region announcing where Jesus had come. The people would immediately carry their sick to that place. It didn't matter, says Mark, if the place was in the villages, cities, or country (6:56).

Apparently, news of the news of Jesus' healing of the woman with the issue of blood had gotten around (Mark

5:25–34). Those who touched the hem of Jesus' garment were made well. But as in the previous example, Mark's point is not that Jesus' clothes were magical. He says that the people "begged Him that they might just touch the hem of His garment." Here we see the simplicity of sincere faith. To beg implies several things. First, it implies a great desire. We don't beg for things about which we are indifferent. Sometimes Jesus asked those He met, "Do you want to be made well?" (John 5:6). What may seem like an unnecessary question is meant to test whether or not people are really fed up with their condition and really desire God's help. Second, begging implies a great humility. Without humility a great cure may be just beyond our reach (cf. 2 Kings 5:11–12). Those who are truly trusting in Christ for all things needful are not too proud to beg.

The second half of Mark 6 reveals a willing Christ. He is willing to teach—we must listen to Him. He is willing to care for our ordinary physical needs—we must trust Him. He is willing to comfort our fears—our hearts must be open to Him. He is willing to heal our deepest hurts—we must be willing to beg Him for help. One of the caricatures of serious religion is a commitment to a stern, prudish God who is reluctant to help and eager to punish. Maybe some of us have struggled with such a view of God. But when we understand that Jesus Christ is the "express image" of the person of God (Heb. 1:3) we get a completely different picture of God. In Christ, we see a God who meets our needs with spectacular sufficiency. He is a God who is willing and able to be for us what we cannot be for ourselves.

## Questions

1. Why does it seem pious to be always busy?

2. How do we cultivate a piety of rest and refreshment (cf. Mark 6:31)?

3. In what way is Christian teaching—whether formal or informal—a demonstration of compassion (cf. 6:34)?

4. How does Mark 6:35–36 speak to the practice of congregational hospitality?

5. What seems to be the main point of Mark 6:42–44?

6. How does it encourage you to know that Jesus "makes continual intercession for us with the Father" while at the same time He "governs us by His Word and Spirit, and defends and preserves us in the salvation obtained for us" (*Heidelberg Catechism*, Q&A 31)?

7. What is the relationship between "fear" and "good cheer" (cf. 6:50)?

8. When is the last time you "begged" anything of God (cf. 6:56)?

1. Bethsaida, where the feeding of the five thousand occurred, is only a few miles from Capernaum.

2. *Belgic Confession*, Article 1.

3. David Murray, "The Most Overlooked Doctrine," accessed December 8, 2014, from http://www.christianity.com/blogs/david-murray/the-most-overlooked-doctrine.html.

4. That Jesus' disciples are said to be heading to Bethsaida both prior to and following the feeding of the five thousand (Luke 9:10) presents some interpretive difficulty. Darrell Bock suggests that Luke is referring to the "city in the tetrarchy of Philip, located on the northeast corner of the Sea of Galilee" while Mark uses a generic name to refer to a distinct locale on the west side of the sea *Luke,* Baker Exegetical Commentary on the New Testament, vol. 1 (Grand Rapids: Baker Books, 1994), 828.

5. Cf. *Heidelberg Catechism*, Q&A 31.

6. William Hendriksen, *Exposition of the Gospel According to Mark*, New Testament Commentary (Grand Rapids: Baker, 1976), 263.

# CLEAN AND UNCLEAN

---▶ ● ◀---

**Mark 7:1–37**

In the Old Testament God instituted a distinction between clean and unclean things (Lev. 11). But of what use is this distinction to us today? In Mark 7 Jesus applies this important biblical teaching to His hearers. In no uncertain terms Jesus says that all of us have become unclean because of our defiled hearts. The good news is that Jesus shows His compassion toward the unclean by making them clean.

The first half of Mark 7 (vv. 1–23) contains the last narrative describing Jesus' focused Galilean ministry. Jesus will be back in Galilee again but not as consistently as before. It is telling, then, that before Jesus exits Galilee, He is subject to yet another attack from the scribes and Pharisees, this time over the issue of ceremonial cleanliness. This is the seventh such confrontation that Mark records.[1] Seven is the Bible's number of fullness. Strikingly, in the next two narratives Jesus ministers among "unclean" Gentiles.

## The Source of Uncleanness (7:1–23)

In this confrontation with the Pharisees Jesus first publicly exposed their hypocrisy. In so doing He provides opportunity for us to examine ourselves and to repent of our hypocrisy.

*The Pharisees' Accusation (7:1–6)*

For true fault-finders, opportunities to criticize are never lacking. A delegation of religious experts who recently arrived from Jerusalem found fault with the disciples for— of all things—failing to wash their hands in the traditional way. As Jerusalem was the capital of the Jewish religion this criticism provides sad commentary on the legalistic bondage (cf. Gal. 4:25) and "slavish doctrine and worship into which [first-century Judaism] had degenerated."[2] The disciples had recently traveled the countryside preaching repentance, casting out demons, and healing the sick only to hear the Pharisees say, "You don't wash your hands right!"

The kind of washing prescribed by the scribes and Pharisees wasn't meant to remove germs but to remove spiritual defilement. The Old Testament did require people to wash after becoming ceremonially unclean (Lev. 15:11). Through the law God was teaching His people the principle of purity. But the Pharisees went beyond God's law and elevated their own law above His, instituting special washings the Bible never required; it is "the tradition of the elders" that the disciples had undermined (7:3, 5).[3] Jesus' response is scathing and should cause us to closely evaluate our understanding and use of tradition.

### Jesus' Response (7:6–23)

Instead of simply defending his disciples for not washing their hands Jesus used Isaiah 29:13 to expose the Pharisees' hypocrisy and legalism. Hypocrisy is the lip service of a disinterested heart. A hypocrite is literally one who wears a mask. The Pharisees wore a mask of religion to cover their lack of true piety. The great danger of religiosity is that one can go through the motions—attempting to placate God with sacraments, church attendance, tithing, and so forth—while wandering far from Him. John Calvin put it well: "Nothing pleases [God] that is not accompanied by the inward sincerity of heart."[4] God calls hypocrites to de-mask by confessing their sins to God and others. God can already see behind our masks. Confession shows that we agree with Him about what He sees.

Jesus also charged the Pharisees of being legalists who teach "as doctrines the commandments of men" (7:7). There is a great difference between law keepers and legalists. Legalists require what God does not require or forbid what God does not forbid, and they make human tradition of greater weight than God. The Bible nowhere condemns tradition *per se.* Traditions can help keep us stable, keeping us from making crazy mistakes on a whim. But they can also blind us from God's will, keeping us from exploring alternatives to our well-worn paths. In an honest moment in *Fiddler on the Roof,* Tevye says, "Because of our traditions every one of us knows who he is and what God expects him to do." Therein lies the problem. We should know who we are and what God expects us to do not through tradition but through Scripture.

The Pharisees' hypocritical legalism is illustrated by the way they understood obedience to parents (7:10–13). The Pharisees taught that monies properly set aside for parental support could be designated as "Corban" (meaning "a gift to God") and then used at one's personal discretion. In denouncing the practice of Corban Jesus got to the heart of filial obedience and obedience in general. To "honor your father and mother" (Exod. 20:12) requires more than legal compliance; it requires heart devotion. In fact, there is no such thing as selfish, reluctant, feigned, or coerced obedience.[5] A legalistic attitude undercuts true obedience by focusing attention more on the rules (and the human audience) than on God. With such a mindset, it is possible to develop an ethic that strains out gnats and swallows camels (Matt. 23:24).

Not surprisingly, Jesus' words offended the Pharisees. Matthew says that the disciples came to Jesus privately saying, "Do you know that the Pharisees were offended when they heard this saying?" (Matt. 15:12). Of course they were offended (cf. 1 Peter 2:8)! The disciples had yet to learn that those who are living contrary to God's Word need to be offended. We must be sensitive toward the weak but strong toward the obstinate and rebellious (Jude 22). By contrast, Jesus tenderly shepherded the people who were not being shepherded by the religious leaders. "Hear Me, everyone, and understand" (7:14). Jesus ministered to the consciences of the multitudes which had been burdened by so many non-biblical, pharisaical stipulations.

Strangely, Jesus' announcement of good news sounds, at first, like bad news. Jesus says that defilement comes from within, not from without (7:14–23). In so saying, Jesus makes clear that the dietary and other ceremonial laws are not binding in the New Covenant. In fact, Jesus makes clear that the distinction between clean and unclean in the Old Testament was primarily meant to teach a spiritual and ethical distinction, not a hygienic one.[6]

Jesus then got to the heart of defilement by listing twelve sins that flow from the heart. He first mentions evil thoughts. Our minds were created to be creative; after the fall, they tend to create evil. Second, Jesus highlights three sexual sins. When Jesus talks about "adulteries" He has in mind "all unchaste actions, gestures, words, thoughts, desires, and whatever may entice one thereto."[7] Closely connected to adulteries is "lewdness," or a failure to bridle sexual or sensual passions, but instead giving free play to perverse impulses.[8] "Fornications"[9] describes sexual deviancy in its most general form. Human sexuality is to be expressed between a husband and his wife. All sexual expressions outside of these bounds are sin. Third, Jesus mentions sins that clearly hurt others. Jesus understands "murders" not only as the taking of life but as malicious harm (Matt. 5:21–22). Sinful hearts also "thieve" or take to themselves what rightly belongs to others. "Deceit" is the selfish use of trickery. "Blasphemy" is injurious speech against God or religion. Fourth, Jesus speaks of three defiling attitudes. "An evil eye" refers to envy, or displeasure over another's gain. "Covetousness" is the unholy desire for what we have not. "Pride" refers to unduly elevated thoughts of self. Finally, Jesus provides the two general terms of "wickedness" and "foolishness" to sum up the list.

Jesus' conclusion is stunning. This list of sins leaves the profound impression that unrinsed hands are the least of anyone's problems! Rather than finding fault with those whose tradition differs from ours we should take inventory of our own hearts. Jesus' exposé demonstrates how wrong it is to impose on the freedom of others; we have our own ugliness to deal with! The good news is that real purity is not only possible but it is promised by God in Christ. With joy we hear God say, "Come now, and let us reason together . . . Though your sins are like scarlet they shall be as white as snow; though they are red like crimson, they shall be as wool" (Isa. 1:18). Real purity is achieved as we repent of our sins and are washed by the blood of Christ. Bring your defiled hearts and hands and exchange them for the perfect righteousness of Christ. In the next two narratives Mark shows two Gentile sinners doing just that.

## The Source of Cleanness (7:24–37)

Mark now begins to write about Jesus' "retirement ministry." From now on Jesus withdraws more and more from the crowds, spending instead more time with the disciples, preparing them for His departure. He also withdraws from Galilee, spending more time in Gentile lands. Some Galileans would never again see Jesus' face, hear His rebukes, or experience His compassion. Eventually they would get back into their routines and forget about His ministry. Many missed their window to come to Him in repentance and faith. For good reason God says, "Today, if you hear his voice, do not harden your hearts" (Ps. 95:7–8). According to God's plan, often when some harden their hearts to the gospel others have a new opportunity to hear it (cf. Mark 6:11). This was the situation for a woman from Tyre, a city situated in Gentile lands on the northeast coast of the Mediterranean Sea.

### The Syro-Phoenician Woman: A Picture of Bold Faith (7:24–30)

Once again Jesus sought peace and quiet, now among people who would have been less affected by His popularity. Again, He could not be hidden (7:24; cf. Matt. 5:14; John 8:12), "For a woman whose young daughter had an unclean spirit heard about him" and requested His help. The woman's request for healing is striking in three respects. First, we notice her humble posture; "she came and fell at His feet" (7:25; cf. Mark 3:11; 5:22–33). Her prostration is a twofold recognition, first of Christ's sovereignty and second of her own inadequacy.

Second, the woman's request is persistent in the face of Jesus' repeated and potentially offensive denial. "She *kept* asking him" (7:26; cf. Matt. 15:23–26). Jesus responds to her persistence with a mini-parable: "Let the children be filled first, for it is not good to take the children's bread and throw it to the little dogs" (7:27). The Jewish people were the children of God's house. He had adopted them, raised them from their days of infancy in the time of the patriarchs, made promises to them (Rom. 9:4), toddled them through the wilderness into the Promised Land, nurtured them by the prophets under the protection of the kings, and endured their rebellious teenage years during the exile. How can Jesus, the bread of life (John 6:35, 48), now give Himself to Gentiles? God's plan was to bring the gospel first to the Jews (Rom. 1:16).

Third, the woman's request was bold. She takes the words of Jesus' parable about bread and daringly tosses them back at Him. "Yes, Lord, yet even the little dogs under the table eat from the children's crumbs" (7:28). She acknowledges herself as an unworthy dog begging for crumbs. She's saying,

"Even the table scraps of your mercy would be sufficient for me." How beautiful! What do we want from God? As a start, we want to have healthy bodies, good social skills, a happy church, a beautiful house, clear skin, reasonable intelligence, community respect, an easy life. This woman says, "Just give me some crumbs!" The one who eats crumbs of God's mercy is still eating the bread of life; because of her faith, the woman's daughter is restored. When we have Christ, we can be content regardless of how little else we have (Heb. 13:5).

*The Deaf and Mute Man: A Picture of Regeneration (7:31–37)*
After leaving Tyre, Jesus met a deaf-mute man in the Gentile territory of the Decapolis. Three times already, in Mark, Jesus has said, "If anyone has ears to hear, let him hear."[10] In the subsequent narrative Jesus asks His disciples, "having ears, do you not hear?" (8:18). According to Jesus having ears is not enough; your ears must be tuned to the voice of God. Now, here is a man who has ears but cannot hear; he has a mouth but cannot speak; a perfect illustration of what Jesus has been teaching.

Today there are tremendous opportunities for the hearing and speaking impaired, including cochlear implants, sign language, and texting. But this man was almost totally excluded from human communication. He had a huge need. At first Jesus' method of responding to the man's need seems strange (7:33). Upon closer inspection Jesus is using a form of sign language to work faith in this deaf and mute man. The man couldn't hear, but he could feel Jesus' fingers enter his ears and touch his tongue. Jesus then looked to heaven to signify to this man from where the healing would come. He sighed to signal His compassion for sinners and regret over sin. Finally, Jesus did something you might not expect. He stood face to face to the deaf man and spoke. "Ephphatha," He said. "Be opened" (7:34). How many people had tried and failed to speak to this man? Jesus spoke one word and the man was totally healed (7:35).

Christ's healing of the deaf-mute illustrates that only God can give spiritual understanding. This man could have slept through a house fire unaware of the shouts of his friends. He could have been in the presence of the most beautiful music and heard nothing. So it is with natural man apart from the healing grace of God; their ears are plugged by depravity (cf. Mark 4:12). God communicates all the time, but until He unstops the ears His voice does not penetrate to the heart. How is your spiritual hearing? If you are spiritually deaf, ask God to give you ears to hear.

When those present saw the miracle they disregarded Jesus' command "that they should tell no one" (7:36). Sometimes we puzzle over why Jesus desired to keep His healings a secret (and why the people often disobeyed). But Christ knew the temperament of the people. They were looking for a physical healer and king. He told them to keep quiet to minimize His popularity. This verse also teaches us to obey God even when He *seems* wrong. It seemed so right to these people to tell others what Jesus had done for them. But Jesus had expressly commanded the opposite. Their actions do not demonstrate enthusiasm, excitement, or uncontrollable gratitude but a failure to submit to God's word.

Every so often someone in Scripture makes a statement that is loaded with meaning beyond that person's understanding.[11] In response to the healing of the deaf-mute the people said, "He has done all things well." They may simply have been expressing their astonishment at Jesus' healing power. But what a statement! Everything Jesus ever did was right. He never had a lapse in judgment. He never did anything out of mixed motives. He never made a mistake. He never committed a little sin. The perfect purity of Jesus is exactly the good news that unclean sinners need to hear.

## Questions

1. Commenting on Jesus' denouncement of the Pharisees' Corban rule, Calvin gives the example of people who considered violating Lent as "nothing less than a capital crime, while theft or fornication is regarded as a venial fault."[12] How does this happen?

2. In what ways might we be guilty of "laying aside the commandment of God" to "hold the tradition of men" (Mark 7:8)?

3. How does Jesus' list of contaminating sins (Mark 7:21–22) compare with the Ten Commandments?

4. The Syro-Phoenecian woman is persistent in seeking Jesus' help for her daughter. Are we pounding on the doors of heaven for those who need God's help?

5. Can you find illustrations from the Psalms (or elsewhere) that encourage the believer to be bold with God?

6. Jesus sighed over the deaf-mute's fallen condition. How should believers sigh over human fallenness?

7. What does Ephesians 4:29 say about how we must use our tongues? Does it suggest also how we should use our ears?

8. How might Mark 5:20 account for the fact that while Jesus was previously asked to leave Decapolis (5:17) on this return trip He is welcomed by those who looked to Him for healing?

1. Mark 2:7, 16, 18, 26; 3:2; 22.
2. John Calvin, *Commentaries on the Epistles of Paul to the Galatians and Ephesians* (Grand Rapids: Baker Book House, 1989), 140.
3. Translations vary on the meaning of the adverb translated "in a special way" in the New King James Version. The point seems to be that the Pharisees were overly rigorous in their washings.
4. John Calvin, *Commentary on a Harmony of the Evangelists, Matthew, Mark, and Luke* (Grand Rapids: Baker Book House, 1989), vol. 2, 253.
5. William Hendriksen, *Exposition of the Gospel According to Mark*, New Testament Commentary (Grand Rapids: Baker, 1976), 277.
6. Cf. Acts 15; Col. 2:16–17; Acts 10:11. Even theonomist R. J. Rushdoony acknowledged that "the primary principle of division is religious, of which the medical and hygienic is a subordinate aspect" and that "the dietary laws are not legally binding on us" (*The Institutes of Biblical Law* (Nutley, NJ: Craig Press, 1973), 300, 301.
7. *Heidelberg Catechism*, Q&A 41; cf. Matt. 5:28.
8. Hendriksen, *Mark*, 288.
9. The Greek word is *pornea*, from which we get "pornography."
10. Mark 4:9, 23; 7:16 (the latter is omitted by some translations).
11. For example, when Caiphas advises the Jewish leaders that "it is expedient that one man should die for the people" (John 11:50). He was saying that it would be better for Jesus to die than for the commotion caused by His teaching to bring problems on the Jews by the Romans. But his statement is inspired by the Spirit to mean much more.
12. Calvin, *Commentary on a Harmony of the Evangelists*, vol. 2, 252.

# PHARISAISM AND DISCIPLESHIP

**Mark 8:1–38**

What does it mean to be a Christian? If you asked this question of an average group of people you would get a number of different answers. "It means going to church. It means believing in God. It means belonging to a religious tradition." Jesus gives a radically different answer. A Christian is a disciple: a student who learns from Jesus by denying himself, taking up his cross and following Jesus.

Situated right in the center of Mark's Gospel, chapter 8 addresses what it means to be a follower of Jesus. The first half of the chapter focuses mainly on a roadblock to true discipleship, namely, spiritual blindness. In the second half of the chapter Jesus presses His disciples to reckon with who He is and to lay everything else aside to follow Him.

## The Danger of Pharisaism (8:1–26)

Suppose you were driving along the interstate. As you approach a blinking roadside sign you see one word: "Beware." The sign has gotten your attention. After a few seconds the letters change to say, "Slippery road conditions." The word *beware* would serve to underscore the gravity of the conditions. At the center of our passage, after feeding another enormous crowd Jesus and His disciples crossed the Sea of Galilee to Bethsaida, a city on the sea's northern coast. On the way, Jesus warned His hearers to "beware the leaven of the Pharisees" (8:15). Just as strings of a spider's web converge in the center, so the several parts of this passage converge on this warning.

*Introducing the Warning*

Don't wonder if you don't understand what Jesus means by "the leaven of the Pharisees." The disciples didn't get it either. It's even harder for us to understand because we are so far removed from the concept of leaven, or yeast. People understood yeast in Jesus' day because they made bread. They understood that bread changed with just a little bit of yeast. As Paul says, "A little leaven leavens the whole lump" (Gal. 5:9). Leaven is the difference between flat and fluffy bread. Yeast cells grow on the sugars of the batter. Dividing and multiplying, they expand the bread by producing carbon dioxide. Jesus uses the word *leaven* to mean something small in quantity which thoroughly pervades a thing and changes it.

By comparing Mark's account with those of Matthew and Luke we can better understand the leaven of the Pharisees. Matthew tells us that Jesus is talking about "the teaching of the Pharisees" (Matt. 16:12). Luke says the Pharisees' leaven is hypocrisy (Luke 12:1). Christ uses the concept of leaven to illustrate a religious approach that can kill true spirituality by creeping in and changing one's whole approach to God. He's not just helping the disciples to detect the faults of the Pharisees but to guard against them in their own lives. In fact, they were already beginning to show frightening signs (Mark 8:17–18). Let's look at a few specifics of this warning, identifying five examples of the leaven of the Pharisees and how we can take heed against it.

*The Specifics of the Warning*

First, Jesus warns against the leaven of spiritual blindness. The Pharisees' blindness to the things of God (8:18) is underscored by their request for a sign (8:11). Ironically, this passage is bookended by signs (8:1–10, 22–26) which the Pharisees were unable to interpret due to their blindness (Matt. 16:3; Luke 12:56). What good is a sign if you can't see? Imagine being asked by a blind person if you could point him in the direction of a certain street sign. The Pharisees' request is equally bizarre. We must beware of trying to pursue the spiritual life without having spiritual eyes. If you don't understand what true religion is all about, if you don't see your sinfulness or the beauty of Christ, if you don't understand what this "gospel" talk is, ask God to give you sight. The healing of the blind man at Bethsaida is a case study in how the Lord grants sight (8:22–26). The man couldn't see, but Jesus gave him vision, healing in stages to show that his restoration was no coincidence.

Second, Jesus warns against the leaven of unrepentance. The Pharisees' lives are case studies in unrepentance. Mark doesn't mention Jonah, but in the parallel passages Christ says, "No sign will be given you except the sign of Jonah" (Matt.16:4; Luke 11:29). Jonah was figuratively raised from the dead to validate his message of repentance. The Pharisees believed everyone needed to repent but them (Luke 15:7). Beware of self-righteous unrepentance. Prayerfully examine your heart in the light of God's Word. Humbly study the sin in your own life from God's perspective.

Third, Jesus warns against the leaven of doubt. He criticizes the Pharisees' demand for evidence (8:11). The Pharisees' religiosity obscured their lack of real trust in God. Jesus was right to deny their request for a sign. Faith takes God at His word. It doesn't test God by seeking signs (Matt. 16:1). Jesus' warning against doubt hits closer to home when He criticized the disciples' concern over their lack of bread. When Jesus mentioned the yeast of the Pharisees, the disciples began to notice their lack of bread (8:16). They doubted the providential ability of Christ. There are several ways we can combat the leaven of doubt. First, we must focus on the promises of God which are the bedrock of the Christian faith (e.g., Heb. 13:5). Second, we should remember the pity of God (8:2). As in days of old God is moved to pity by the groaning of His people (Judg. 2:18). Third, we ought to reflect on the power of the God who can turn seven loaves of bread and a few small fish into a meal for thousands. Fourth, we need to remember (8:18) the providence of God. The disciples could look back over God's providential dealings with them and say, "Thus far the LORD has helped us" (1 Sam. 7:12). Jesus' disciples probably still had the miraculously created bread in their stomachs but already doubted. How quick we are to forget.

Fourth, Jesus warns against the leaven of materialism. Materialism is a denial of the supernatural and its practical implications. When Christ mentioned leaven, the disciples immediately thought about bread. They reveal affinity with the Pharisees, who were consumed with material things. Pharisaism puts a religious gloss over our natural inclinations; humanism with a veneer of religion. We too are prone to think in material terms. Counselors will tell you that the problem a counselee presents rarely reflects the deeper spiritual issues. We think we're stressed because of our busyness; the deeper problem may be that we place activities above spiritual disciplines. We think we're depressed because we have no friends; the deeper problem may be that we put too much stock in human acceptance. Be sensitive to the spiritual reality of life. Jesus asked, "Is not life more than food and the body more than drink?" (Matt. 6:25). "Seek first the kingdom of God and his righteousness" (Matt. 6:33).

Fifth, Jesus warns against the leaven of legalism. Legalism is the reduction of religion to law keeping. Sometimes Christianity is presented as simply a better way to live; the gospel as simply a better set of rules. Could this be why so many people today have no need for the church? The church has rules; the world has rules. Neither seems to keep them!

Christianity is not about living by a better set of rules. It is about experiencing a relationship with the one who kept all the rules for us. It is about growing in love with God and learning to hear and respond to His voice as a lovely thing. If we hold on to even a little bit of legalistic works-righteousness, we are in danger of missing Christ (Gal. 2:21).

Pharisaism has not gone extinct. All of us are tainted with it. Sadly, the typical remedy for this problem is "Stop being a Pharisee," which itself is a Pharisaic approach. The real solution to Pharisaism is to follow Jesus all the way to the cross; to receive healing for spiritual blindness, unrepentance, doubt, materialism, and legalism from His precious blood. It's this solution that Mark presents in the second half of chapter 8.

## The Call to Discipleship (8:27–38)

Jesus showed His integrity by explaining to His would-be followers the cost of discipleship. Up to this point it had been relatively exciting to follow Jesus. The crowds enjoyed the social, diaconal, and intellectual benefits of following the Teacher. But with every step toward the cross Jesus made plain that discipleship is not about fellowship or food. It's not about having your ears tickled. Discipleship is costly.

Jesus was leading twelve men, most of whom were trying to follow Him but were still learning how. He had around Him a larger group of people who were still figuring out who Jesus was and whether or not they wanted to follow Him. Most of us fall into one of those two categories. So, what does discipleship mean to us?

### The Path of Christ (8:27–33)

To follow someone means first to understand who he or she is and where that person is going. Before unveiling the radical call to discipleship Jesus invited the Twelve to reflect on who He is (8:27–30). This is one of the most important questions we can ever consider. Peter's declaration that Jesus is the

Christ (v. 29) is very significant. The christs, or "anointed ones," of the Old Testament were appointed and equipped for an official position or task (e.g., 1 Sam. 16:13). The three main official positions were those of prophet, priest, or king. These Old Testament messiahs were typical, or representative, of the coming Messiah. In his baptism, Jesus was anointed by the Father to be His official prophet, priest, and king (Mark 1:9–11; Luke 4:18). As prophet He perfectly reveals to us God's will. As priest, He sacrificed His own life for sinners and continues to intercede for those whom He is saving. As king, He governs and protects His blood-bought subjects.[1]

After clarifying the nature of His being, Jesus revealed the nature of His ministry. His announcement was so startling that Peter rebuked Him (8:32): "The Son of Man must suffer many things." Jesus here introduces a new phase in His ministry. From this point on Mark makes it increasingly clear that Jesus is headed for the cross.

Twice before Jesus had used the title "Son of Man" to refer to Himself (2:10, 28). From this point on He will use it much more frequently (it is His favorite self-designation). Jesus probably used this title because it carried the least amount of baggage in Jewish minds. It also aptly communicates both His lowliness and exultation. The Son of Man is a "human figure, ministering, suffering, dying,—though already clothed with authority in the midst of his . . . [humiliation, who will] return clothed in glory."[2] The title "Son of Man" is the perfect way to introduce Jesus' future path. Jesus would suffer many things, being abandoned by friends, derided by critics, and tortured by enemies (8:31). As the stone the builders rejected, Jesus would be scorned by the leaders of the old system who had no place for a suffering savior. As the propitiation for our sin (1 John 2:2) He would be crushed under God's devastating wrath.

If Jesus had stopped here, His message would have been tragic. But He went on. He would rise again on the third day. The way up is down. The way to glory is riddled with trials. "Weeping may endure for a night, but joy comes in the morning" (Ps. 30:5). This mingling of hope with hurt helped prepare the disciples for what Jesus would say next.

### The Path of the Christian (8:34–38)

A true disciple is one who walks as Jesus walked (1 John 2:6). In His call to discipleship Jesus clearly outlines our path.

To follow Christ down this path we first need to know who Jesus is. That's why He asked His disciples, "Who do you say that I am?" (8:29). The way you answer this question will profoundly shape your life. Is He your Prophet? Do you hang on His every word? Is He your Priest? Are you trusting in His blood alone for your salvation? Is He your King? Are you diligently learning to submit to His loving rule in every area of your life? Your answers to these questions are eternally significant. Disciples of Jesus have a desire to come after Christ (8:34) because He is worth following. Disciples are not ashamed of Christ or His words (8:38; cf. Rom. 1:16). No one is ashamed of his most valuable possession.

Second, to be disciples we must place a value on our soul. Is the eternal prosperity of your soul worth risking on a life of predictability, pleasure, or pandering to the desires of men? What can you give in exchange for your soul (8:37)? As you place an eternal value on your own soul, everything that would challenge your heavenly hope becomes a vile enemy.

Third, disciples must deny themselves. Our natural glory-seeking tendency is a great hindrance to effective crossbearing. But the gospel turns on its head the basic self-glorifying drive of natural man. When God changes our hearts we are no longer driven to please ourselves. But we still war against the flesh. Therefore we must deny ourselves. Calvin said, "We are God's own; therefore let every part of our existence be directed toward him as our only legitimate goal."3

Fourth, disciples must take up their cross. Dietrich Bonhoeffer wrote, "Christ bids us to come and die."4 The cross represents the sufferings of Christ that we experience (Gal. 6:17). To take up one's cross is to embrace Christian suffering as part of God's plan for our lives. Like Christ we learn obedience as children through crossbearing (Heb. 5:8). Crossbearing also compels us to more fully crave God's perfect justice while we live in a perverse world (Gen. 18:25). Only as we truly take up our cross will we relish the apostle's claim that believers are crucified with Christ (Gal 2:20).

The call of discipleship is radical! In Mark 8 Christ speaks both of His suffering and the suffering of the Christian. But Christ did not suffer and die merely as an example of how we should suffer and die. He suffered and died as the ultimate self-denier for those who cannot go that far. He took up His cross for those who too often cast off their crosses. What a comfort that Christ calls us to follow Him as the Great Shepherd who supplies all our wants, answers all our fears, and promises us a place at His eternal banquet (Ps. 23).

## Questions

1. How is it possible that the disciples could so quickly forget Jesus' miraculous ability to feed the hungry (compare Mark 6:37 with Mark 8:4)? Can you relate?

2. Contrast Mark 8:4 with Mark 8:8. What is God here teaching His people?

3. In what ways must we take special heed to the leaven of the Pharisees (8:15)?

4. Why is Jesus' question in Mark 8:27 so important?

5. How does Jesus' rejection by the elders, chief priests and scribes (8:31) demonstrate that Jesus cannot simply be added to the worldview of an unbelieving person?

6. Is it possible that we sometimes (more subtly) imitate Peter in rebuking Jesus (8:32)?

7. How are failing to take up one's cross (8:34) and being ashamed of Christ (8:38) related?

8. Reflect on some ways that discipleship can be practiced in community in ways that it cannot be practiced in isolation from others.

1. Cf. *Heidelberg Catechism* Q&A 31.
2. B. B. Warfield, *The Lord of Glory* (Grand Rapids: Guardian Press, n.d.), 29–31.
3. John Calvin, *The Golden Booklet of the True Christian Life* (Grand Rapids: Baker, 1952), 26.
4. Dietrich Bonhoeffer, *The Cost of Discipleship* (New York: Macmillan, 1963), 99.

# THE TRANSFIGURATION, FAITH, AND UNBELIEF

▶ ◦ ◀

**Mark 9:1–29**

In 2010, newscaster Brit Hume made a public appeal to golfer Tiger Woods to "turn to the Christian faith." In response, columnist Tom Shales spitefully compared Hume with "Mary Poppins on the joys of a tidy room, or Ron Popeil on the glories of some amazing potato peeler."[1] For many people, the idea of trusting in Christ is insignificant— at best.

In Mark 9, Jesus' disciples caught a brief glimpse of His heavenly glory—and saw just how life-changing Christ can be. Considering the weighty trials that we face, we need to experience the glory of God shining in the face of Jesus Christ (2 Cor. 4:6).

"Glory" is one of the most powerful words that the Bible uses to describe God. "Glory" means "significance" or "weightiness." Glory is the opposite of trivial or unimportant. Christian disciples need to know that God is glorious. Clearly, Jesus' original disciples needed to hear this. They had been faithfully following Him for some time. They believed He was the Christ, but they had just heard some sobering words about discipleship and cross bearing (Mark 8:34). Perhaps some of them had considered quitting. Was following God worth it? Was the cost too high? The disciples needed an impression of the glory of God to conquer their doubts.

Jesus explained, at the beginning of this chapter, that some of the people in His audience would see the kingdom of God present with power before they died (9:1). Many people probably thought Jesus was talking about an earthly political kingdom. Instead, Jesus was taking about the kingdom of righteousness that He brought through His words and works. Six days after making this mysterious statement Jesus led Peter, James, and John to a secluded mountainside and revealed the kingdom of God present with power. As He showed His glory the disciples were powerfully convinced that Christ is worth following regardless of the cost.

Christ's timing couldn't have been better, for as the disciples descended from the mountain they immediately faced their helplessness and their utter need for God's power.

## A Mountaintop Experience (9:1–13)

The humble form Christ assumed at His birth can be misleading. Isaiah sums it up: "He has no form or comeliness; and when we see Him, there is no beauty that we should desire Him. He is despised and rejected by men, a man of sorrows and acquainted with grief. And we hid, as it were, our faces from Him" (Isa. 53:2b–3a). But mystically united to this humble frame is a divine nature of pure glory which was briefly revealed to three disciples.

### *"Jesus Was Transfigured" (9:2)*

The verb Mark uses to describe Jesus' transfiguration is *metamorphao,* the word from which we get "metamorphosis." In an instant, His whole form changed. The glory of God, which had been veiled by Christ's flesh, was temporarily revealed. He shone brighter than the reflection of the snow on a sunny winter day (cf. Matt. 17:2).

Jesus' transfiguration reminds us that on the night of His birth, heaven opened, "and the glory of the Lord shone" around the shepherds (Luke 2:9). The song of the heavenly hosts began with this word, "Glory!" Not only does Christ's shining form remind us of His first arrival from heaven, but also it reminds us of His second coming. The last verse of the previous chapter (8:38) says that the Son of Man is coming in the glory of His father. Do not be deceived by Christ's humility. He is meek. But He is also a glorious king. He suffered at the hands of sinful men, but He was not dragged to His death. He went willingly to pay the price for the sins of His beloved people. On this mountain the disciples briefly glimpsed beyond the humanity of Christ, and they were delightfully terrified (9:6). They learned firsthand that Jesus is not to be trifled with.

*Jesus Entertained Visitors*

Christ's transfiguration was marked by the appearance of Moses and Elijah, two prominent Old Testament figures who, significantly, are both referenced in the last verses of the Old Testament (Mal. 4:4–6). God commanded His people to "Remember the Law of Moses, My servant, which I commanded him in Horeb for all Israel, with the statutes and judgments" (Mal. 4:4). At the transfiguration God caused Moses to be engulfed in Christ's glory on the mountain. The great law giver Moses paid homage to the great law keeper, Christ, confirming that Christ is the prophet like unto Moses predicted more than a millennium earlier (Deut. 18:15, 18–19). Moses' visitation makes clear that law is important, but until you submit to Christ you cannot be a law keeper.

Joining Moses on the mountain was Elijah. Malachi said that he would come first and restore all things (Mal. 4:5–6). Elijah would turn the hearts of God's people through repentance. Although Elijah had already come, so to speak, in John the Baptist (Mark 9:13; Matt. 17:13), he now stood face to face with the one to whom repentant sinners must turn to find restoration.

The last word Malachi wrote after mentioning Moses and Elijah, the last word of the Old Testament, is "curse." Luke tells us that Moses and Elijah spoke with Jesus about His "exodus" (9:31) by which He would remove the curse of His people.

Not surprisingly, Peter didn't know how to handle the situation—so he decided to open his mouth just wide enough for his foot to fit. "Let us make three tabernacles" for Jesus, Moses, and Elijah, respectively (9:5). Did Peter seriously think that these three needed the protection of chintzy manmade shelters? Jesus' body was effusing divine glory. Moses and Elijah had been brought from before the throne of God for this special meeting. And Peter talks about building them booths? Peter often reminds us of the spiritual discipline of silence. Solomon writes: "Do not be quick with your mouth . . . let your words be few" (Eccles. 5:2, NIV). With due respect to Peter, because he didn't know what to say (9:6) he should have said nothing or asked a simple question like "Master, what shall we do?" Mark records no answer to Peter's ridiculous statement. Instead, God the Father takes center stage.

### Jesus Was Recognized by God

The Father's statement, "This is My beloved Son, hear Him!" is similar to the voice heard at Jesus' baptism. But there are significant differences. This time the mountain was engulfed by a cloud, reminiscent of God's glory which led the people from Egypt to Horeb (Exod. 13:21; 24:15). God's voice forcefully complements the theme of glory and power communicated by the transfiguration. "Hear Him!" Jesus was the prophet Moses and Elijah anticipated. His words carry the absolute authority of God. The Father explicitly refocuses attention from Moses and Elijah to His Son: "*This is My Son!*" Whatever glory belongs to Moses or the Law, or Elijah and the prophets, must bow to Christ (cf. Matt. 5:17).

After God's speech, and with symbolic importance, Moses and Elijah disappear (9:8).

"Now as they came down from the mountain, He commanded them that they should tell no one the things they had seen, till the Son of Man had risen from the dead" (9:9). If the disciples hadn't understood what had just happened, why would anyone else? Christ's transfiguration would later drive the apostolic witness: Even in the midst of His humiliation they had been "eyewitnesses of His majesty" (2 Peter 1:16–18). God often teaches us things that we'll understand only later. His perfect patience and timing are a great comfort to God's children in times of discouragement. Christians serve a God of infinite glory. In the present age Christ's glory is somewhat veiled but nonetheless real.

The glory of God represents our hope for positive change. The word for "transfigured" is used only twice outside of this event. In both instances the word refers not to the transfiguration of Christ but to the transfiguration of the Christian. The first instance is Romans 12:2. We are to be transfigured, or transformed, by the renewing of our minds. We study the Word of God so that the Spirit of the glorified Christ will change us from the inside out.

The second passage is even more striking. "But we all, with unveiled face, beholding as in a mirror the glory of the Lord, are being transformed into the same image from glory to glory, just as by the Spirit of the Lord" (2 Cor. 3:18). As we see the absolute brilliance of God in Christ, as we are struck by the sheer significance of our God, we are being transformed into the same image from glory to glory. Do you want to be changed into something new? God wants us to know that change comes not by implementing a few tips or strategies but by beholding His glory.

This is a lesson some of the disciples were about to learn in the face of personal inability.

## I Think I Can't, I Think You Can (9:14–29)

One of the most famous moralistic tales elevating the power of positive thinking is *The Little Engine That Could.* In the story a little blue engine is the only one willing to attempt to pull a stranded train over difficult terrain to its destination. The little blue engine accomplishes the seemingly impossible task by repeating the mantra "I think I can, I think I can." As cute as this little story might be, all of us know (or will know soon enough) that thinking positively about our own abilities cannot guarantee success.

But if we change that little train's motto just a bit we have a fairly simple summary of Mark's message in the second half of Mark 9. The father in this story faces the great burden of finding relief for his demon-possessed son. But he doesn't say, "I think I can, I think I can." Instead he says to Jesus, "I think *I can't,* I think *you* can." Remembering the glorious God we serve, this should be our attitude as we face the problems in our life.

### The Problem (9:14–22, 28–29)

The healing of this boy begins with a problem. Actually, Mark interacts with several layers of problems. This is a great way to tell a story because it is suggestive of the great story of mankind as well as the story each of us experiences every day.

First, there was the child's problem of the demon (9:17–18a, 21–22). This poor boy was frequently seized by a spirit that sought to destroy him by casting him into the fire and into the water. It had probably left him with few, if any, friends. His life was ruined. As such he paints a very good picture of natural man with no way to deliver himself.

Second, there was the disciples' inability to exorcise the spirit which apparently prompted a dispute with the scribes (9:14–16). The scribes were thrilled to point out the disciples' failure. They may have taunted the disciples by asking, "Where are your powers now!" The disciples were befuddled by this very question (9:28). According to Jesus, the disciples couldn't cast out the spirit because of their little faith (Matt. 17:20; Luke 17:6). As evidence of their little faith the disciples had approached this problem apart from prayer and fasting (9:29). We may wonder that the disciples tried to solve a problem that was obviously beyond their control without seeking God's help. But maybe the disciples had been thinking the way we often do. "This isn't *really* beyond my control. I know what to do." But all human effort is impotent without the God's energizing power (John 15:5). Through fasting we humble ourselves before God while making requests through prayer. Fasting stimulates prayer by exposing personal weakness. Calvin paraphrases Christ's response to the disciples' inability: "You seem as if you were engaged in a mock-battle got up for amusement; but you have to deal with a powerful adversary, who will not yield till the battle has been fought out."[2] Are we really so different from the faithless disciples? Do we approach great need with prayer and fasting or without?

Third, there was the general problem of unbelief. Jesus used this occasion to get at the most pervasive problem of all. In denouncing the "faithless generation" (9:19) Jesus seems to be speaking most specifically, though not exclusively, against the scribes. They had seen so many signs, but here they capitalize on one failure to justify their unbelief. Like the scribes we tend to focus on life's problems often forgetting all the powerful signs of God's grace we have seen. Unbelief enlarges problems and minimizes God's power and provision.

### The Heart of the Matter: Faith (9:23–24)

In the face of this great problem the father of the demon-possessed boy asked for two things: compassion and help (9:22). But he prefaced these two requests with a bit of skepticism. He didn't say, "You can do anything!" but, "*If* you can do anything." He did believe that Christ could help (otherwise he wouldn't have asked), but doubt lingered. Unbelief is severely debilitating. In response Jesus explained that faith in God swings open the door of possibilities: "If you can believe, all things are possible to him who believes" (9:23).

This needy father answered with one of the simplest expressions of humble faith found in the Bible. He demonstrated faith without arrogance or presumption. It is a saying that every child of God can resonate with: "Lord, I believe; help my unbelief!" (9:24). This father's profession helps us to combat unbelief by honestly examining ourselves and resolutely committing ourselves to Christ's care. When we take a careful look at our faith we must admit weakness. In general, believers believe. But there are specific areas in which we are prone to doubt. This man had doubts that his son could be healed. For years he had seen him ravaged by this spirit. He had lost hope that anything could help. There might be areas in your life in which you have relinquished hope in God. Have you become content with your anger or rudeness, suspecting that God cannot provide a solution? Do you doubt that God could improve your marriage? Identify your areas of unbelief and ask for God's help.

### The Resolution (9:25–27)

On many occasions God had used the disciples to cast out similar demons. But on this occasion they could do nothing. In fact, their inability to resolve the problem drew a huge crowd and sharp disagreement. The disciples' failure put Jesus on center stage (9:25). When Jesus cast out the unclean spirit, the child fell down as if dead; so powerful is the strength with which Satan clings to the souls of those he is seeking to ruin. Christ's power is greater. "Christ has come to bridle [the] rage [of Satan]."[3]

Luke provides a powerful connection between the two narratives in this story; Jesus healed this boy *the day after* the transfiguration (Luke 9:37). It seems that the disciples who failed to cast out the demon were not with Christ on the mountain.[4] They lacked an overwhelming sense of His power and glory. What an advantage we have in the full panorama of revelation. Because of His glory Christ is more than able to give us victory over sin and Satan.

## Questions

1. Reflect on the following: Something like Christ's transfiguration takes place every time a person is converted.

2. In what way are the Father's words in Mark 9:7 a missionary charge to His disciples in every age?

3. How might Christ have been strengthened by His Father's words?

4. Why do you suppose Jesus asked the question recorded in Mark 9:21?

5. What do you think about the father of the demon-possessed boy confessing his faith and unbelief in public, with a loud voice and tears?

6. Identify areas in your own life where unbelief is stronger than faith.

7. Why do you suppose Christ took the boy by the hand and lifted him up after the demon was driven from him? What does this teach us about Jesus?

8. Has fasting become the forgotten discipline of the confessing church? If so, how should it be recovered?

1. Accessed on January 26, 2015, http://www.washingtonpost.com/wp-dyn/content/article/2010/01/04/AR2010010403101.html.

2. John Calvin, *Commentary on a Harmony of the Evangelists, Matthew, Mark, and Luke* (Grand Rapids: Baker Book House, 1989), 2:327.

3. Calvin, *Harmony of the Evangelists*, 323.

4. William Hendriksen, *Exposition of the Gospel According to Mark*, New Testament Commentary (Grand Rapids: Baker, 1976), 345.

# SELF-LOVE AND DISCIPLESHIP

————————————▶ ● ◀————————————

**Mark 9:30–50**

It's been said that self-esteem is the single greatest need facing the human race today. One prominent pastor, in defending this thesis, has defined self-esteem as "pride in being a human being."[1] A sincere study of Scripture, however, seems to suggest that self-esteem, rather than being our greatest need, might be part of humanity's problem. In Mark 9 Jesus teaches us how truly to care for our never-dying souls—not by thinking more highly of ourselves but by becoming servants.

In the second half of Mark 9 Jesus continues to teach His disciples how to follow Him. Broadly speaking, the principles highlighted in this passage can be boiled down to one: Christ's disciples must learn to deal with their natural overabundance of self-love. Excessive self-love keeps Christians from being effective followers of Jesus because true discipleship is characterized by self-denying servitude (v. 35). This message might not stimulate greater pride in being human. But, blessed by God, it will make us more like the One we have been called to follow.

## Disciples Disregard Greatness (9:30–37; 10:13, 16)

Soon after the transfiguration Jesus and His disciples passed through Galilee on their way to Capernaum. The disciples must have been just out of earshot of Jesus as they walked.

They certainly didn't want Him to hear what they were
discussing, namely, who among them would be the greatest
(vv. 33–34). The disciples' conversation topic is startling
when you consider the context.

*A Startling Context*
First, the disciples had just been humiliated by their failure
to cast out a deaf and dumb spirit from a young boy (Mark
9:14–29). Luke informs us that after Jesus performed the
exorcism "they were all amazed at the majesty of God"
(Luke 9:43). How could the disciples argue about personal
greatness after being awe-struck by God's majesty in contrast
to their failure? Probably in the same way that we can
transition from a service of divine worship to service of
self on any given Sunday. One of the purposes of corporate
worship is to astonish us with the greatness of God. In
worship we affirm that "the Lord is great in Zion, and He
is high above all the peoples" (Ps. 99:2), including ourselves.
Weekly we come to "Mount Zion and to the city of the living
God, the heavenly Jerusalem, to an innumerable company of
angels, to the general assembly and church of the firstborn
who are registered in heaven, to God the Judge of all, to the
spirits of just men made perfect, to Jesus the Mediator of
the new covenant, and to the blood of the sprinkling that
speaks better things than that of Abel" (Heb. 12:22–24).
The regularity and spiritual intensity of our worship provide
a context in which concern for personal greatness should
appear utterly insane.

Second, the disciples' verbal battle for greatness follows
directly on the heels of Jesus' second passion announcement
(vv. 30–32). Luke says that "while everyone marveled at
all the things which Jesus did," pertaining to the exorcism,
"He said to His disciples, 'Let these words sink down into
your ears, for the Son of Man is about to be betrayed into
the hands of men'" (Luke 9:44). "And they will kill Him"

(Mark 9:31). Christ says, "I will be betrayed and killed." The disciples said, "We want to be great." The incompatibility of these statements is partially explained by Luke: "But they did not understand this saying, and it was hidden from them so that they did not perceive it; and they were afraid to ask Him about this saying" (Luke 9:45). For the believer, the completed canon of Scripture and the internal testimony of the Holy Spirit provide a context which should militate against a quest for personal greatness.

*A Sobering Rebuke*

Before Jesus even opened His mouth to rebuke the disciples they were rebuked by their consciences. "They kept silent" because they were ashamed of their thoughts (Mark 9:34). Conscience is a powerful aid to the Christian life. As Puritan Nehemiah Rogers said, a conscience well-informed by the Word of God will prove a friend and faithful witness for the Lord but an adversary against man.

Knowing their thoughts Jesus got right to the point: "If you want to be great in My kingdom, then be a servant." Disregard greatness. Striving for greatness has no place in the church because it breaks with the example of Jesus, who gave up the glory of greatness to serve (Phil. 2:5–8). But striving for greatness is also inconsistent with trusting in Christ. When we trust in Christ we are saying, "There is no good in me (Rom. 7:18); that's why I need Him." How can we then turn around and find prideful satisfaction in our own status? Christ prophesied that He would suffer and die for self-centered people like us so that we could find ourselves in Him (Col. 3:4).

To make His point that true greatness shines through humility (Matt. 18:4), Jesus used the visual aid of a child (cf. 10:13–16).[2] Being a member of His kingdom means showing attention to those who are usually considered less important. In fact, the way believers treat children can be telling. Sometimes we yell at children when they displease us. Or we furrow our brow as we scold them for some misdeed. We treat children and other less powerful people with less dignity than we treat our peers. Our desire for greatness rears its ugly head with those who are weaker than us, often children. Disciples don't just help themselves; they help those who are needy, like children.

## Disciples Avoid Sectarianism (9:38–41)

After Jesus' object lesson John said something that might well have been meant to deflect Jesus' criticism of the apostles. Instead, he provides another example of that kind of self-love which is debilitating to Christian discipleship. "Teacher, we saw someone who does not follow us casting out demons in Your name, and we forbade him because he does not follow us" (v. 38). Clearly John did not properly anticipate Jesus' response: "Do not forbid him," He said (v. 39).

Instead, Jesus forbade an intolerant attitude toward dissimilar believers. The disciples focused on themselves ("he does not follow us"); they should have focused on Christ. The disciples' intolerance reveals their selfish ambition. John Calvin explains: "Christ declares that we ought to reckon as friends those who are not open enemies."[3] Paul shared Jesus' point of view. "The important thing is that in every way, whether from false motives or true, Christ is preached. And because of this I rejoice. Yes, and I will continue to rejoice" (Phil. 1:18, NIV).

*Intra-church Sectarianism*

Within our congregations we too often take offense at the way others are trying to follow Christ. We might disagree with a pastor's leadership methods. We might not care for the style of worship. We might have our own ideas about how the Sunday school should operate. But when we understand the Spirit's diversity in distributing spiritual gifts we will think twice about breaking fellowship over such matters. Paul points out the absurdity of expecting uniformity in the church. "If the whole body were an eye, where would be the hearing? If the whole were hearing, where would be the smelling? But now God has set the members, each one of them, in the body just as He pleased. And if they were all one member, where would the body be?" (1 Cor. 12:17–19).

We might also have a tendency to exclude new people in our church because "they are not one of us." God expects us to treat newcomers with the same sort of love that long-time members have come to expect from each other. In fact, the "outsiders" that God brings into our midst should be our greatest priority (Deut. 10:18–19). Dietrich Bonhoeffer, alluding to Christ's words in Matthew 25 (vv. 41–45) said, "The exclusion of the weak and insignificant, the seemingly useless people, from a Christian community may actually mean the exclusion of Christ."[4] We are prone to think "this is my church." But three times in this short dialogue the phrase "in Christ's name" is used. The church is Christ's.

*Inter-church Sectarianism*

The kind of narrowness here forbidden by Jesus is also evident in the way believers view other camps within the boundaries of Christian orthodoxy. Can we say that Christian groups who disagree with some of the positions we take are "on our side" (v. 40)? We ought not be surprised to find a multiformity among true Christian churches. "We read in the ancient writers that there were manifold diversities of ceremonies, but that these were always free [to differ]."[5] This diversity is clearly evident even in churches in the New Testament. "We know, moreover, what manner of churches the churches in Galatia and Corinth were in the apostles' time, in which St. Paul condemns many and heinous crimes; yet he calls them holy Churches of Christ" (1 Cor. 1:2; Gal. 1:2).[6] Further clarification is provided in the seventeenth-century

*Westminster Confession of Faith.* This confession explains that "this Catholic (or universal) church has been sometimes more, sometimes less visible. And particular Churches, which are members thereof, are more or less pure, according as the doctrine of the gospel is taught and embraced, ordinances administered, and public worship performed more or less purely in them. The purest Churches under heaven are subject both to mixture and error" (25:4, 5).

Notwithstanding their current negative reputation, denominations are a way that Christians with different convictions can recognize the legitimacy of other groups without having to face the near-impossible task of harmonizing each difference. The disciples were a denomination of sorts. But there were other Christians who did not follow Jesus as they did. Jesus said because they were trusting in Him they were on His side. All Christians are on the same team! Those who work for Christ have a reward in heaven (v. 41); should they not be received as members of one church? Jesus commends a certain level of cooperation and fellowship among distinct theological traditions. Rather than being unduly negative toward other traditions, let us strive to maintain our own doctrinal and moral purity while reaching out to those who love the Lord and His Word.

Jesus has already used a child to teach about discipleship. In the final passage in the chapter He does so once more, this time on the danger of coddling sin.

## Disciples Cut Out Sin (9:42–50)

Knowing that His disciples are inclined to exalt themselves and look down on others, Jesus concluded this teaching session by emphasizing the need for personal holiness. The church is a "holy congregation of true Christian believers."[7] All those who follow Jesus regard sin as a danger to be avoided and a cancer to be removed.

Jesus' method for dealing with sin is not the "cut back" method but the "cut off" method. If your eye sins, pluck it out. If your hand causes you to sin, cut it off. If television causes you to sin, you too may have the satisfaction of throwing it out a window. If you are involved in pornography, tell someone and purchase some accountability software. If you aren't taking drastic measures against sin, then you aren't fighting sin with Christ-like tenacity.

Jesus gives two reasons for taking sin seriously. First, we must fight sin for the sake of others (v. 42). Our sins cause others to sin. Young children quickly learn to imitate their older siblings. Children learn from their parents. As scary as this might be, the apostle Paul saw this principle of imitation as a critical component of discipleship. He told the Corinthians, "Imitate me, just as I also imitate Christ" (1 Cor. 11:1). Testifying before a governor and a king Paul had the commendable audacity to say, "I would to God that . . . all who hear me today, might become both almost and altogether such as I am" (Acts 26:29). Conversely, our sin minimizes our effectiveness in the world. If we are engaged in the sins of our culture, then we will be salt-less (v. 50). We will have nothing to offer the world. Christians who live in sin demonstrate a practical hatred of a watching world.

Second, believers must fight sin for their own sake. Jesus repeatedly spoke about the fires of hell as a deterrent to ungodly living (vv. 43, 45, 47). The person who does not deal with sin is better suited for hell than for heaven, because hell is for those who love to sin. The end of sin, if allowed to flourish, is death (James 1:15). William Jenkyn said, "There is nothing destroyed by sanctification but that which would destroy us."[8]

Underlying each of these three narratives is one central theme. You and I tend to act as if we are the center of the universe. We are so wrapped up in ourselves. This is why we want to be great. This is why we take offense at those who are different from us either on a personal or a church level. And this is why we persist in sins that pleasure our flesh.

How do we remedy this self-love? Jesus' emphasis on hell helps us answer that question. Thoughtful reflection on hell should rattle a believer out of sinful self-absorption. Imagine the most painful experience of your life and how much relief you experienced when it was over. There is no such relief in hell. Biblical references to hell are like so many warning signs emphasizing the memorable words of John Owen: "Kill sin or it will be killing you." These warning signs should also stir us to communicate the gospel of Christ to those who are not yet saved.

But, as always, the Bible's warnings ultimately point us to Christ. As self-absorbed sinners we must ask Christ to fill the center of our lives. We naturally see ourselves as God. When Christ comes into your life, He begins to move into that center. And as He does He relieves us of all the burdens that self-love creates. When Christ is at our center we don't have to be great. We don't have to get angry over being disrespected at work or at home. Those who are united to Christ by faith God respects because of His respect for His Son. What else matters? When Christ is at our center we don't have to take offense at people who do things differently. God, through the gospel, says to us, "I'll cover you when you get offended. I've borne a million times more offense than you ever will, and I did it for you." The person who trusts in Christ can say, "Those people differ from me, but Christ makes that okay. After all, I'm very different from Christ, and yet He loves me." When Christ is at our center we don't have to cling to our sins for satisfaction. Jesus becomes more important to us than our stinking sins. The only way to get over self-love is to grow in love with the only one who can give us the kind of love we really need.

## Questions

1. Why were Jesus' words in Mark 9:31 so easily misunderstood by the disciples?
2. What are some ways that we strive to be first, contrary to Jesus' words in Mark 9:35?
3. Why were children such suitable object lessons for Jesus (Mark 9:36–37; 10:13–16)?
4. In what way might Jesus' teaching against sectarianism confront us?
5. What does it mean to cause a little one to stumble (Mark 9:42)?
6. Can you provide additional contemporary examples that fit with Jesus' teaching in Mark 9:43–48?
7. Why do you suppose verse 44 is repeated two more times (vv. 46, 48)?
8. Can sin be defeated simply by taking drastic physical measures against it? Explain.

1. Robert Schuller, *Self-Esteem: The New Reformation* (Waco, TX: Word, 1982), 19.

2. Jesus didn't have to send for a child; they were part of the group of disciples that followed Jesus. This fact does not prove the propriety of infant baptism, but it does support a covenantal approach to discipleship of which infant baptism is an appropriate expression.

3. John Calvin, *Commentary on a Harmony of the Evangelists, Matthew, Mark, and Luke* (Grand Rapids: Baker Book House, 1989), vol. 2, 373.

4. Dietrich Bonhoeffer, *Life Together* (San Francisco: Harper & Row, 1954), 38.

5. *Second Helvetic Confession*, 17:15.

6. *Second Helvetic Confession*, 17:12.

7. *Belgic Confession*, Art. 27.

8. William Jenkyn, *An exposition upon the epistle of Jude: Delivered in Christ-Church* (London: John Childs & Son, n.d.), 12.

# MARRIAGE, MATERIALISM, AND MINISTRY

▶ ◦ ◀

**Mark 10:1–52**

In his book *City on a Hill,* Phillip Ryken asserts that "a Church for post-Christian times is a teaching church." He goes on to say that "the only church that will survive in post-Christian times is a church with a passion for God's Word."[1] As elsewhere, in Mark 10 Jesus sets a pattern for the teaching church (v. 1).

There are a few things you can't miss about Jesus' teaching. He taught with authority. His teaching was saturated with love (v. 21) and mercy (vv. 47–48). He didn't seem to stick to a script but taught according to the needs of the audience. He answered questions and responded to circumstances. He didn't avoid difficult issues. As He and His disciples marched toward Jerusalem Jesus tackled three difficult issues: marriage, money, and ministry.

## Discipleship and Marriage (10:1–12)

The question of divorce is extremely relevant given the failure rate of marriages today. A recent study reveals that 33 percent of Americans who marry will divorce. This statistic seems to show little variance between believing and unbelieving demographics. George Barna, the director of the study, noted that Americans have grown comfortable with divorce as a natural part of life. "There no longer seems to be . . . a stigma attached to divorce; it is now seen as an unavoidable rite of passage."[2]

Even with the changing cultural norms regarding divorce, the topic still evokes strong emotions in the church. This was true in Jesus' day as well. The question, "Is it lawful for a man to divorce his wife" was put to Him as a test (10:2); it seems to have no good answer. If Jesus said yes, His opponents could accuse Him of advocating divorce. If He said no, they could say that He was ignoring the law of Moses, which allowed for divorce. Jesus' approach to this topic is extremely helpful. The Pharisees focused on the exception to the rule—divorce—while Jesus focused on the institution of marriage.

## The Exception

Jesus began to answer the Pharisees' question on divorce by asking what the Old Testament had to say about it. The text to which the Pharisees appeal is Deuteronomy 24:1–4. Commentators do not always agree on the grounds that Moses here provides for divorce.[3] What is clear is that in the Old Testament divorce was not difficult. Even so, this provision was given, not as an indulgence to capricious men but as a protection to undervalued women. A man who would dishonor his marriage vow at least had to provide a certificate stating that the marriage was over and that his ex might marry again and not be left destitute.

But Jesus' point is that divorce was permitted (not commanded) due to hardness of heart. "Divorces were permitted, not because they were lawful, but because Moses had to deal with a rebellious . . . nation."[4] The overwhelming evidence in the Old Testament is that God does not delight in divorce (Mal. 2:13–17). In the New Testament, the divorce loophole is tightened. There are only two biblical grounds for divorce. A spouse who has committed adultery has dissolved the marriage and set the other at liberty (Matt. 5:31–32).[5]

Paul also seems to allow for divorce in the case of radical desertion (1 Cor. 7:10–16). While there is some disagreement on this point,[6] it is clear that the grounds given for divorce in many marriages today are not scriptural.

## The Rule

Jesus brought up grounds for divorce to touch on possible exceptions that prove the rule. God's rule for marriage is lifelong monogamous, heterosexual commitment (10:6). Jesus elaborates on this rule by first pointing out that there was no divorce before the Fall: "From the beginning it was not so" (Matt. 19:8). This is a powerful ethical principle. In Genesis 2 God opens a window into perfect humanity's family life: Adam and Eve remained exclusively faithful to each other. Anything other than this perfect picture is a deviation from God's intention.

Second, Jesus elaborates on the "one flesh" principle (10:6a, 8). Men and women are two unique fleshes, two distinct but complementary parts of humanity. They were made to fit each other, physically, emotionally, and spiritually. In marriage two fleshes become so joined that they can no longer be called two but one.

Third, Jesus teaches the rule of marriage by comparing marriage with the filial bond (10:7–8). We may wonder, "What could be stronger than the bond between parents and their children?" Jesus' answer is, "The marriage bond." For the purpose of marriage a man shall leave his father and mother to be united to his wife.

Fourth, Jesus teaches the rule of marriage by emphasizing that God makes the marriage (v. 9). Something happens in marriage that goes beyond the two people involved. God joins man and woman together into one flesh. Who are we to separate that union?

One advantage of studying human failures, divorce being just one example, is that we see more clearly the integrity of

God. "You have played the harlot with many lovers," says the Lord. "Yet return to me . . . for I am married to you" (Jer. 3:1, 14). Such commitment on God's part unshakably grounds the faith of His followers.

## Discipleship and Materialism (10:13–31)

At this point in His public ministry, Jesus was looking for committed disciples. As He briskly approaches His darkest hour He spoke candidly about what it means to enter the kingdom of God as a disciple (vv. 15, 23). A disciple is a person who follows Jesus to learn from Him in order to be like Him (Luke 6:40). At the heart of Mark 10 Jesus echoes His earlier call to "Come, take up your cross and follow Me" (cf. 8:34). The main lesson is: Discipleship is a total sacrifice. One of the great obstacles to discipleship is materialism. In this passage Mark gives both positive and negative examples of discipleship as it touches on the theme of materialism.

*Examples of True Discipleship*

Peter exemplifies all true disciples when he says, "We have left all to follow you!" (v. 28). Jesus agrees. They have left houses, families, and lands for the sake of the gospel (v. 29). Disciples realize that no sacrifice is more important than following Jesus. A few verses earlier Jesus compared discipleship with childhood (10:13–16). Children often demonstrate total commitment. There is nothing a loving child wouldn't give up for a loving parent. My little child would spend all the money in her bank account to buy me a cheeseburger if that's what would please me. Even following painful discipline godly children remain lovingly committed to their parents.

*An Example of Non-Discipleship*

By contrast, the rich man of verses 17–22 exemplifies all who despise discipleship. In response to his question, "What shall I do that I may inherit eternal life?" Jesus uses the commandments as a checklist to identify the heart-idol that was keeping the rich young ruler from committing to Christ. He found it in his riches. To this ruler, money was more important than God. For now, at least, "he went away sorrowful" knowing that he could not be a disciple. He knew that he wasn't just a bad tither; he wasn't a Christian! Some of us may be more deceived. What is it that we will not let go of? Consider the following list of heart-checking demands: Give up your career plans to raise a godly family. Ask for a demotion at work so that you can spend more time with your kids. Give at least 10 percent of your income to God's work. Stop overeating. Give up electronic devices that lead you into temptation. God isn't necessarily calling us to do all these things. But He does demand that we put nothing before Him, whether reputation, relationships, comfort, control, or security.

Jesus speaks specifically here to the discipleship stumbling block of money. Jesus is not saying that wealth and religion are antithetical; the Bible's patriarchal and monarchial history disproves such a notion. This man was not too rich. He just loved his riches too much. The same might be true of you whether you make twenty thousand, two hundred thousand, or two million dollars per year. Wealth is such a dangerous idol because it can provide us with a sense of freedom, identity, and security—three things that come only truly through the gospel.

The rich man's failures can also help us to identify false standards of discipleship. Sometimes we might take a "simple majority" approach to discipleship. Doing more Christian than non-Christian things does not make you a disciple. Beware also of a "big-ticket item" approach to discipleship. Sadly, those who with an unbelieving heart do such "big-ticket" activities as worshiping, tithing, witnessing, or volunteering will still hear Christ say those dreadful words: "I never knew you" (Matt. 7:23).

### The Radical Nature and Reward of Discipleship

When Christ hit His disciples with God's view of discipleship they were literally driven to despair: "Who then can be saved?" (v. 26). If you have listened to Jesus' teaching and thought, "I'm the model of discipleship," then you have utterly missed the point. Jesus was clear when He said, "With man, it is impossible" (v. 27). "But," says He, "not with God; for with God all things are possible."

Jesus said if you have left all for Christ you will not miss anything. Jesus speaks of a hundredfold gain in this life and eternal life in the age to come (vv. 29–30). These rewards are not without cost (v. 30); it's just that the cost is worth it. Jim Elliot knew the cost of discipleship. He was a bright, well-educated man who gave up everything he had for Christ. He was killed, along with four others, while attempting to evangelize a brutal South American tribe. But because he had already done the math of discipleship he could write, "He is no fool who gives what he cannot keep to gain that which he cannot lose."

Such a perspective prepares us to hear Jesus' final hard theme of this chapter.

### Discipleship and Ministry (10:32–52)

It is said that repetition is the mother of all learning, a fact Jesus obviously knew well. In this passage, for the third time in as many chapters, Jesus predicted His approaching suffering (vv. 32–34). Twice before these words had gone over the disciples' heads (8:32; 9:32) so He lovingly repeated them. He was preparing His disciples for the unimaginable. With every passing day, Jesus was getting closer to the cross. He was "going up to Jerusalem" (v. 32). Up to this point Mark mentions Jerusalem in the context of people coming *from* Jerusalem; often Jesus' enemies. But now He is going up to Jerusalem to face His enemies for the sake of His people.

In this passage Jesus gives us a beautifully succinct statement expressing the purpose of His ministry. "The Son of Man did not come to be served, but to serve, and to give His life a ransom for many" (10:45). At the heart of this passage is the service of Christ. Three distinct but related aspects of this service are highlighted in the last half of Mark 10.

*The Service of Christ Predicted (10:32–34)*

This first point will be very uncomfortable if we understand it. In our minds examples of service might include raking the widowed neighbors' leaves or clearing the table after a meal. But the service of Christ is intimately connected with suffering. In Jerusalem Jesus would experience betrayal, injustice, mockery, degradation, and physical pain. Jesus is the one whom Isaiah predicted would be "despised and rejected by men" (Isa. 53:3). Significantly, His passion prediction forms the theological basis for His teaching on service and sets the pace for understanding Christian suffering (cf. Mark 10:38–40). Christian service is a calculated giving of one's life, patterned after Christ's service. Many of the disciples who were following Jesus to Jerusalem would endure similar fates as their Master.

*The Service of Christ Reflected (10:35–45)*

As Jesus expressed His humiliation, the disciples expressed their desire for exaltation. All twelve of them were guilty in this regard, not just the two who had asked for personal favors (v. 37). When the ten heard about what the two had done they were angry. They didn't want someone else asking for (or receiving) anything they couldn't have.

When we say, "That's not fair," what we often mean is, "I'm upset that I missed out." We tend to have such an egocentric concept of greatness. As such we miss opportunities to make God's kingdom great. Christians need to see themselves as part of something bigger than themselves. But like the disciples we often only care for how this kingdom benefits us.

In the face of the disciples' failure Jesus teaches several things about service. First, service entails real suffering. Jesus equates the ministry of the Christian with His own ministry. The disciples would be baptized with His baptism and drink the cup that He drank. Second, Jesus says that true disciples refuse to rule with a heavy hand. Jesus knows that the disciples have a tendency to lord it over others. We've already seen how they have abused their leadership position (cf. 10:13; 9:38; 6:36). Jesus says that leaders in the church lead without making those they're leading feel oppressed. Christian service is selfless. Bishop J. C. Ryle said, "Let all who desire to please Christ watch and pray against self-esteem."[7] Christian service is kingdom-focused, people-oriented, and self-abasing.

### The Service of Christ Demonstrated (10:46–52)

Sometimes godliness is sooner caught than taught. Jesus, while on the way to the cross, stopped to heal an ordinary beggar. That is service in action! Jesus teaches that mercy—voluntary, unconstrained care for those who are hurting—is at the heart of Christian service. Bartimaeus had no right to Christ's mercy. Neither do we. But to God's glory Christ came to serve hurting sinners who had completely de-merited His help.

As with Christ's service to Bartimaeus, so Christian service is a combination of word and deed. Jesus neither drops a few coins in Bartimaeus's cup, nor does He simply say, "Your sins are forgiven." He heals Bartimaeus physically and teaches him to keep his faith fixed upon the Savior. Bartimaeus's response paints a striking portrait of true discipleship: "Immediately he received his sight and followed Jesus on the road" (v. 52).

## Questions

1. According to Ephesians 5:22–33, how does human marriage communicate the gospel?

2. What light do such passages as Jeremiah 3 and Ezekiel 16 shed on marriage and divorce?

3. How can Jesus' teaching on divorce be applied to people in the following walks of life: single, married, divorced?

4. How does the rich young ruler's answer to Jesus' questions betray a superficial understanding of obedience (v. 20)?

5. How can wealth be dangerous to true religion?

6. How is God's long-suffering shown in the fact that Jesus announces His passion on three different occasions?

7. How can we avoid ambition in its older definition (inordinate desire for honor) while embracing ambition as it is understood today?

8. What can we learn from Bartimaeus?

1. Philip Ryken, *City on a Hill: Reclaiming the Biblical Pattern for the Church in the Twenty-first Century* (Chicago: Moody Publishers, 2003), 25.

2. Accessed on February 11, 2010, from http://www.barna.org/barna-update/ article/15-familykids/42-new-marriage-and-divorce-statistics-released.

3. There has always been some question about what it means for a man to put away a wife upon the discovery of "some uncleanness in her" (v. 1). Many interpreters understand this to mean nearly anything. In fact, quarrels in marriage often begin over such small things. Some of these quarrels end in separation.

4. John Calvin, *Commentary on a Harmony of the Evangelists, Matthew, Mark, and Luke* (Grand Rapids: Baker Book House, 1989), vol. 2, 378.

5. Under the Old Testament administration an adulterer would be stoned, clearly ending the marriage (Deut. 22:22).

6. Some see Paul's counsel here as merely freeing the deserted from the bondage of having to try to abide with the deserting spouse. Others see this as a legitimate ground for divorce and therefore remarriage (cf. *Westminster Confession of Faith*, 24.6).

7. J. C. Ryle, *Expository Thoughts on the Gospels: Mark* (Carlisle, PA: Banner of Truth, 1985), 218.

# THE COMING OF THE KING

---

**Mark 11:1–12:12**

When, in AD 70, future Roman emperor Titus marched on Jerusalem with four legions of soldiers he decimated the Jewish population and destroyed the stunning, newly constructed temple built by Herod the Great. Some forty years earlier another King had entered the city. He brought no sword or shield, but only a small group of fisherman and whatever ragtag crowds might have followed Him from the surrounding countryside. He made no overt declaration of war. Nonetheless, in His triumphal entry Jesus shook the city. The responses He evoked from both friend and foe offer important insights into how we should respond to the King of kings.

Beginning in chapter 11 Mark records the second major phase in Jesus' ministry, often referred to as Passion Week.[1] The intensity of the narrative increases while the pace slows. Almost 40 percent of Mark's Gospel focuses on one week of Jesus' life. For good reason do Christians place special emphasis on Passion Week.

## Jesus Makes a Royal Entry (11:1–10)

The town of Bethany, on the eastern side of the Mount of Olives, would be the staging area for Jesus' triumphal entry, which, notably, took place on the tenth of Nisan, lamb selection day (cf. John 1:29).[2]

*Preparation for the Entry (11:1–6)*

It is critical to see Jesus' triumphal entry as patent fulfillment of prophecy (cf. Matt. 21:5). Zechariah 9:9–10, which foreshadows the event, describes the Messiah in terms of joyfulness, peace, lowliness, justice, dominion, and salvation. These verses also include such unmistakable markers as the crowd's shouting and the use of the colt, both of which Jesus clearly fulfills.

John tells us that at the time the disciples failed to connect Zechariah's prophecy with the fulfillment which took place before their eyes. But after "Jesus was glorified, they remembered that this had been written of Him and been done of Him" (John 12:16). Sometimes we reflect on Bible events in a spirit of wistful romanticism: "If only we had been there, how strong our faith would be." The disciples were there, and they didn't get the connection. But we, having the luxury of complete revelation and the abundant outpouring of the Spirit, "have the prophetic word confirmed" (2 Peter 1:19).

In terms of immediate preparation, the disciples were sent to secure the colt upon which Jesus would ride. Jesus gave detailed instructions, which, as expected, came to pass exactly as He had said. As the owner of the cattle on a thousand hills (Ps. 50:10), Jesus—with perfect propriety—commandeered a young donkey (v. 2) which He had prepared for just this occasion. Still, so as not to give offense the disciples were to insure the colt's return (v. 3). He who had divine right to all things still paid due respect to the law.

*The Entry (11:7–10)*

Christ's entry into Jerusalem was a public demonstration of His humility. A large city to begin with, Jerusalem would have been overrun with an influx of Passover visitors. In addition, Jesus had begun to attract a large following, especially after raising Lazarus from the dead (John 12:12, 18). Given the high-profile context, the manner of Jesus' entry is stunning.

He rode in, not on a glistening, battle-ready stallion but on a borrowed donkey. Sitting upon a crude clothes-saddle Jesus unassumingly plodded His way through the city street, lined as it was with coats and palm branches. Up to this point, Jesus had constantly warned the crowds not to make His heavenly royalty known (John 6:15). He knew that such a commotion would be a precursor to His death. But now, in the shadow of the cross, the words of Zechariah 9:9 take shape before every watching eye: "Behold, your king . . . lowly and riding on a donkey."

The crowd rightly read the scene as a call to worship. Above the din of the mob the words from Psalm 118:25–26 could be heard loud and clear.

> Save now, I pray, O Lord;
> O Lord, I pray, send now prosperity.
> Blessed is he who comes in the name of the Lord!
> We have blessed you from the house of the Lord.

This psalm was written to commemorate the Passover and the Israelite exodus from Egypt. It was, therefore, perfectly suited to honor the Deliverer who was greater than Moses. When we learn to see Christ as our delivering King the response will be heartfelt, unashamed, Spirit-energized worship. Jesus said that if His disciples had kept silent the stones would have cried out (Luke 19:39–40). Sadly, the teachers of the law and the religious leaders—those who should have welcomed Jesus with the greatest enthusiasm—became stone-silent at this call to worship. Conversely, Matthew tells us that the next day, children who had gathered in the temple were repeating the crowd's song: "Hosanna to the Son of David!" (Matt. 21:15). Jesus humbly but triumphantly entered Jerusalem to the praise of His disciples, including children.

Because He came during Passover, an event that memorialized the Jews' deliverance from Egypt, many onlookers wrongly anticipated that Jesus would deliver them from their own oppressors, the Romans. What they missed is that the first Passover served also as a symbol of deliverance from sin. Appropriately, Christ's triumphal entry symbolizes His present spiritual rule over His people and His power to deliver His own from the enemy's tyranny. But we should not expect Christ to cure all our political or social problems here and now; such an expectation imports into the present age God's plans for the age to come (cf. Col. 1:20). But as He rules our hearts He frees us from an insatiable desire for carnal pleasure, and the shame and hopelessness that always follow. Because of His power and love we can know that He'll answer us every time we cry out, "Save now!"

Christ's triumphal entry anticipates His future comprehensive rule. This event is a window into the age when Christ will be received by eager hearts in heaven. This is what we look forward to when we pray for God's kingdom to come (Matt. 6:10).

## Jesus Judges Fruitlessness (11:11–26)

Jesus' kingly entry captured everyone's attention. While in the spotlight Jesus would finish His work as prophet by teaching the people, and as priest by dying for their sins. He would begin His teaching in the morning. But He first engaged in a little reconnaissance. In verses 11–24 Mark masterfully intertwines two narratives in which Jesus inspected and judged a fig tree and the temple.

### Jesus Inspects the Temple (11:11)

Jesus' cleansing of the temple was not the result of sudden and rash impulse. The night before the cleansing He had entered the temple and "looked around at all things." What He saw fully warranted His later actions. What if Jesus slipped into the worship service in your church and "looked around at all things"? What would He think about the things we do to distract ourselves during sermons that we feel are too long, about Bibles remaining closed during much of the service, about the lethargic mumbling we sometimes try to pass off as singing? Or, would he be honored by heartfelt worship? The apostle John tells us that Jesus is "in the midst of the seven golden lampstands" (Rev. 1:13). He does witness what takes place in His churches (v. 20).

As the hour was already late, Jesus went to Bethany to rest, no doubt thinking about what the temple had become. Truly, the glory had departed (Ezek. 10:18).

### The Barren Fig Tree (11:12–14)

The next morning, while on His way from Bethany to Jerusalem Jesus grew hungry. Up ahead He spotted a fig tree, which upon closer inspection bore no figs. In response Jesus said to it, "Let no one eat fruit from you ever again" (v. 14). Jesus has been criticized for judging a fig tree for fruitlessness during the fruitless season (v. 13). But Jesus inspected the tree looking for evidence of the onset of fructification. He found nothing but leaves. This tree was not going to bear fruit. Earlier, Jesus had told a parable about a fig tree which had been barren for three years (Luke 13:6–9). Understandably, the owner was unwilling to waste time and resources on such a useless tree. Jesus compared these trees and the people of Israel, who had been given all the benefits necessary to bear fruit. Fruitless but otherwise healthy-looking trees symbolize the faith of hypocrites. Theirs are "the abundant leaves of a boastful yet empty profession."[3] Notably, Jesus' judgment against the fig tree is His only miracle of judgment[4] and His last miracle recorded by Mark. Indeed, the ax is already laid at the root of fruitless Israel (cf. Matt. 3:10). Leaving the fig tree, Jesus and His disciples proceeded to the temple.

### The Cleansing of the Temple (11:15–19)

If we understand Jesus' cursing of the fig tree, His actions in the temple will be quite clear. The temple bustled with religious activity but produced little true piety. Without Christ, "Judaism is a dead and fruitless religion; a monument of divine judgment."[5]

The temple had been built for the purpose of worship. Its sheer size was awe-inspiring. It covered close to a million square feet and was longer than three football fields. It was as beautiful as it was large, exquisitely detailed. But what was meant for worship had become commercialized. Auctioneers sold sacrificial animals at exorbitant prices. Currency exchangers provided proper Jewish coin for the tithe while handsomely helping themselves in the process. Intolerant of these distractions, Jesus cleansed the temple, blocking off "all traffic across the temple courts. Everything came to a standstill."[6] Jesus is foreshadowing the reality that this temple would be made obsolete in Himself (John 2:19; Heb. 9:11). The animals which Jesus drove out would soon no longer be necessary. The Lamb of God who takes away the sins of the world was fast approaching the heavenly altar (John 1:29).

After clearing the temple, Jesus rebuffed Israel's lack of evangelistic zeal. If God calls His temple a house of prayer for the nations (v. 17), then His people should care about the nations (cf. Ps. 67). Jesus' quotation of Isaiah 56:7 reveals Israel's self-absorbed neglect of the nations. The Gentiles' court had been annexed by greedy money changers. The temple had become a sort of good luck charm which the people exploited in a fruitless attempt to alleviate their screaming consciences (cf. Jer. 7:11).

*The Shriveled Fig Tree and Prayer (11:20–26)*
On their way back to Jerusalem the following day the disciples were amazed to see the cursed fig tree already withered. Jesus used this object lesson to teach on the power of believing prayer. One impediment to powerful prayer is a conscience soiled by grudges (vv. 25–26; cf. 1 Peter 3:7). Until

we lovingly, humbly, and patiently deal with conflict our prayers will be hindered. Through forgiveness we resolve not to hold other's sins against them, either in thoughts, word, or actions.

## Jesus Confirms His Authority (11:27–12:12)

After Jesus had cleared the temple, the scribes and chief priests met to hatch a plan to destroy Him (11:18). It should not surprise us to read, therefore, that as soon as Jesus entered the temple the Jewish leaders confront Him on the issue of authority.

### Jesus' Authority Questioned (11:27–33)

Recalling Jesus' actions from the previous day, representatives from the Sanhedrin (made up of the chief priests, scribes, and elders; v. 28) got right to the point: "Who gave you the authority to do these things?" The question of authority is legitimate. God promises strict judgment on those who pretend to speak on His behalf (Jer. 14:14–16). But His opponents revealed their bias against Jesus in two ways. First, His authority *had* been attested by many miracles. They might not have approved of Jesus, but God clearly did. Second, their question seemingly has no good answer. Without divine credentials, Jesus had no right to teach. But if He claimed that His authority came directly from God, in their minds He would be guilty of blasphemy.

Knowing the Sanhedrin's insincerity, in response Jesus asked His own question: "The baptism of John—was it from heaven or from men?" (v. 31). Jesus is not being evasive. If the Jewish leaders had honestly answered Jesus' question, their own would have been answered too. Everyone acknowledged that John's baptism was from heaven—and John testified of Christ. In fact, it was while John was baptizing Jesus that God spoke from heaven saying, "This is my beloved Son, in whom I am well pleased." Jesus' question was easy. When the leaders of Israel claimed not to be able to answer, they were lying. They believed that John had just as much divine authority as they attributed to Christ—none. But they knew that such an answer wouldn't pass public muster (v. 32). Because the Jewish leaders refused to deny publicly Jesus' authority, Jesus went right on teaching. He treated their reluctance to follow through on their challenge as tacit recognition of His authority.

*Jesus' Authority Affirmed (12:1–12)*
Jesus then told a story of an owner who planted a vineyard and leased it to tenants in exchange for a portion of the harvest. Refusing to part with their produce, the tenants harmed and even killed the owner's rent collectors, including his own son. As a result the owner vowed to destroy the tenants and give the land to others. This parable, which was clearly aimed at the Jewish leaders, served two purposes. First, it affirmed that Jesus was indeed sent by God the Father and does possess the authority about which the Jewish leaders asked. Second, it reinforced Jesus' point that Israel was not a fruit-bearing church.

The vineyard was an allegory for the Old Testament church (cf. Isa. 5:1–5). God had given the Jews every opportunity to grow and bear fruit. Despite His tender care the Jewish establishment remained barren, exhausting God's patience. God would not endure their fruitlessness forever. Instead He would judge the Jewish leaders and give His church to the charge of other vinedressers (literally, "tenant farmers" or "sharecroppers").[7] To flesh out that metaphor, in the New Testament age believers, and especially ministers and elders, are sharecroppers of the church of God. We not only benefit from church membership but are also charged by God to make His church fruitful and multiply it. We are stewards, not consumers. Christian ministers are fruit collectors who teach the people of God how to bear fruit to the Lord and urge them in this duty (Rom. 10:15).

Jesus concluded His teaching by explaining how we can build the kind of life that will be accepted by our Owner. Christ is *both* the Cornerstone and the Rejected Stone who would soon be killed and cast out of the vineyard.[8] The stone rejected by the builders of the Old Testament church would be the very support stone of the New Testament church. In what way is your life built on the rock of Christ? Are you building merely on Judeo-Christian values, reminiscent of the values of Jesus' enemies? Or are you building on the only Cornerstone, Jesus Christ?

## Questions

1. Recall how the children present at Christ's triumphal entry picked up the disciples' song of worship (Luke 19:39). How should this event inform us about the opportunities we have to influence our covenant children?

2. In what ways might churches and families today fail to treat children as disciples of Jesus?

3. How does 1 Corinthians 3:16–17 relate to Jesus' inspection of the temple in Mark 11:11?

4. Take a moment to consider whether you have "anything against anyone." If so, "forgive him" (Mark 11:25).

5. Why would the Jewish leaders be offended that in the temple, Jesus had preached the gospel (cf. Luke 20:1)?

6. Can you think of an example where it would be wise to answer a question with a question, as Jesus does in Mark 11:30?

7. What can we learn about "agnosticism" from Mark 11:31–33?

8. How does the Jews' response to Jesus' parable of the wicked vinedressers (Mark 12:12) teach us about conviction without repentance?

1. Identifying the days on which certain events of Passion Week took place is challenging. For example, some scholars place the triumphal entry on Monday while others place it on Sunday.

2. William Hendriksen, *Exposition of the Gospel According to Mark*, New Testament Commentary (Grand Rapids: Baker, 1976), 553.

3. Herbert Lockyer, *All the Miracles of the Bible: The Supernatural in Scripture, Its Scope and Significance* (Grand Rapids: Zondervan, 1961), 236.

4. Lockyer, *All the Miracles of the Bible*, 235.

5. Lockyer, *All the Miracles of the Bible*, 237.

6. Jakob Van Bruggen, *Christ on Earth: The Gospel Narratives as History* (Grand Rapids: Baker Books, 1998), 209.

7. The significant continuity between the Old Testament and New Testament church is shown in that God does not cultivate a new vineyard but gives it over to different tenants. This fact has implications regarding the practice of both the initiatory and continuing signs and seals of the covenant (baptism and the Lord's Supper), as well as for worship, ethics, and a host of other disciplines.

8. Ironically, Jesus' quotation (from Ps. 118:22–23) comes from the same context as the song which the Palm Sunday crowd sang.

# TEMPLE TEACHING (1): TRICK QUESTIONS

———————————▶ ● ◀———————————

**Mark 12:13–44**

It's been said that the only bad question is the one we don't ask. But asking questions can be intimidating. You might wonder if you are the only one who doesn't know the answer to your question. What if you have to explain your question and end up confusing and embarrassing yourself? Sometimes it's a relief to hear someone else ask the question you had in mind but couldn't ask.

In Mark 12, three important questions are raised. We can be glad we weren't the ones to ask them, so long as we learn from the answers.

After clearing the temple, in the days leading up to His crucifixion, Jesus was questioned by three groups of religious leaders. They hoped to trip Him with their questions, giving them leverage with the crowds to put Him to death. They questioned Him on three major issues: the legality of Roman taxation (12:13–17), the reality of the resurrection (12:18–27), and the priority of the commandments (12:28–34). When the interrogation was over, "no one dared question him" (12:34). Their plan had failed. From this point "the chief priests and the scribes sought how they might take Him by trickery and put Him to death" (14:1).

## Taxes (12:13–17)

It's no wonder that taxes have been compared with death. Will Rogers quipped: "The only difference between death and taxes is that death doesn't get worse every time Congress meets." Few issues can stir up stronger feelings than taxes. The same was true in Jesus' day.

*The Question and Answer*

The question, "Should Jews pay taxes to Caesar?" (vv. 14–15), was put to Jesus by the Pharisees and Herodians, two ostensibly unlikely bedfellows. The Pharisees were scrupulous, formal observers of the law. The Herodians were prototypical "cultural Christians" who lived worldly lives with a mere façade of religion. As followers of Herod Antipas's dynasty, the Herodians reaped sordid gain through their support of the Roman government. Content with the status quo, the Herodians were naturally Jesus' political enemies. In this passage, worldliness and legalism unite in their rejection of Christ.

Before posing their politically charged question, Jesus' antagonists slather on a generous dose of patently bogus praise (12:14). Of course, as they said, Jesus *is* the true Teacher who makes plain the way of God without showing favoritism. The problem is, the Herodians didn't believe what they said—and Jesus knew it (v. 15). The Herodians were "spies who pretended to be sincere" (Luke 20:20) to "catch Him in his words," testing Jesus (Mark 12:13; 15) as Satan had earlier (1:13). Supporting Roman taxation was social suicide. However, if Jesus opposed Roman taxation the Jews could deliver Him up to the "authority and jurisdiction of the governor" (Luke 20:20).[1] Wisely Jesus answered with few words (cf. Prov. 10:19). Instead, He gave an object lesson using a Roman denarius, the image and inscription of which affirmed Caesar's right to levy taxes. The questioners were astounded at God's wisdom: "Render to Caesar the things that are Caesar's, and to God the things that are God's" (v. 17). What could they say?

*What Should We Make of This?*

Jesus gives several principles for sorting out the knotty relationship between God and government.

First, Jesus teaches us to respect civil authorities. Jesus could have made His point about taxes in a less respectful way, but He doesn't. It's tempting to believe that only good government, duly elected by the people, deserves our honor. But Caesar wasn't voted into office by popular demand. Rome annexed Palestine by force and ruled with an iron fist. Still, God's people must honor authority (1 Peter 2:17). One way we do so is to pay for the support of an organized society with police and military protection, reasonably good roads, courts, etc. We pay taxes not only out of duty and conscience (Rom. 13:5–7) but also to avoid the shame of delinquency. As a rule of thumb, we should pay every penny that is required and not a penny more.

Second, Jesus teaches us to honor God. Everything in this world bears the impression of God. As Abraham Kuyper said, "There is not one square inch of the entire creation about which Jesus Christ does not cry out, 'This is mine! This belongs to me!'" As we look in a mirror we should repeat Jesus' question, "Whose image and inscription is this?" God's people are made in His image; in baptism we are inscribed with His name. We must render ourselves to God.

On its obverse side the denarius featured the head of the emperor Tiberius with the inscription "Tiberius Caesar Augustus, son of the Divine Augustus." On the reverse side: "High Priest." Caesar sought his own glory. God promises that those who honor Him will be honored more highly than Caesar.

Third, Jesus teaches us to neither confuse God with government nor radically divorce the two. There is a problem when phrases like "in God we trust" and "support our troops" become nearly synonymous. We sometimes have to make hard choices between obeying God and Caesar (Acts 5:29). Still, as John Calvin reminds us, obedience to authority is always joined to the fear of God.[2] Romans 13 presents government as a physical arm of God on earth. This was true in Jesus' day under Tiberius and in Paul's day under Nero. It's still true today.

With little chance to catch His breath, Jesus was quickly assaulted with another trick question, this time from the Sadducees.

## The Resurrection (12:18–27)

Those who believe in a resurrection often wonder what it will be like, especially in terms of important relationships. Will I know my children? Will I have the same friends? Will I still be married to my same spouse when I get to heaven? Behind these questions is the bigger question, the one asked by the Sadducees: "Is there a resurrection at all?" The way that we answer is eternally significant (1 Cor. 15:12–19, 29–32).

### The Question (12:18–23)

The Sadducees were the sect from which the high priests were drawn. Their monopoly on the priesthood provided impetus to eliminate Jesus, especially as He threatened their control of the temple. The Sadducees believed only in the law of Moses (the first five books of the Bible). They denied the resurrection because they thought it isn't taught in those books.

The Sadducees' question is linked to God's provision of a kinsman redeemer. One of the primary purposes of marriage is the perpetuation of a godly seed (Gen. 1:28). In Deuteronomy 25:5–6 God provided a law to help ensure that a man's family line would continue if he died childless. The man's widow was to marry his closest kin and the firstborn of that relationship would be considered the deceased man's son, redeeming his name. The story of Ruth and Boaz is an example of the kinsman redeemer principle in action. Based on this principle the Sadducees dreamed up a scenario which, in their minds, makes the resurrection absurd. If a woman has been married to seven men, whose wife will she be in heaven? An example of a woman who had married twice (not seven times, the biblical number of completeness; cf. Matt. 18:21) would have sufficed. The Sadducees' insincere and exaggerated question probably got them a few laughs.

### The Response (12:24–27)

Jesus responds rather sternly. He begins and ends His answer by saying, "You are (greatly) mistaken" (vv. 24, 27).

The two reasons that the Sadducees got off track touch on many of our own problems, as well. First, the Sadducees had elevated reason above revelation. "You do not know the Scriptures" (v. 24). Regardless of what you think about the resurrection, what does the Bible say (cf. Gal. 4:30; Rom. 4:3)? We need to apply this same question to all the issues of life ranging from interpersonal relationships to biological engineering. We believe the "Holy Scriptures fully contain the will of God, and that whatsoever man ought to believe unto salvation is sufficiently taught therein."[3]

Second, Jesus says that the Sadducees did not know the power of God (v. 24). They had imagined a problem that, to them, was bigger than God. How could God raise the dead with all the resulting marital complications? Numerous additional complications could easily be raised. But the Apostles' Creed begins, "I believe in God the Father, Almighty, maker of heaven and earth." If God created heaven and earth, surely our problems are well within His power.

Having deconstructed the Sadducees' faulty logic, Jesus proceeded to answer the question. There will be no marriage in heaven (v. 25).[4] God created marriage to meet certain needs which are foreign to heaven. First, marriage answers the human need for companionship. Marriage exists because "it is not good for man to be alone" (Gen. 2:18). In heaven there will be no sense of "alone." Second, marriage provides for the perpetuation of a godly seed (cf. the kinsman redeemer principle). But "where there are no burials, there is no need of weddings."[5] Third, marriage helps prevent fornication. Marriage is the appropriate context for expressing natural and appropriate sexual desire. There are no illicit sexual desires in heaven.

Jesus then provided biblical evidence for the resurrection, courteously using the second book of Moses. His argument hinges on the tense of the verb "to be" in Exodus 3 (vv. 3, 15). If Abraham, Isaac, and Jacob are dead and gone, God should have said, "I *was* the God of Abraham, Isaac, and Jacob." Because he says, "I *am* their God," they must still be alive. With these fathers God made an everlasting covenant which death cannot extinguish. The souls of all departed saints are alive and well, awaiting the resurrection of the body.

Behind this interaction between Jesus and the Sadducees lies a profound reality: Jesus is our kinsman redeemer. In the words of Thomas Boston, before the fall "our nature was in a . . . fruitful condition." With the fall came spiritual death and "an absolute spiritual barrenness, as to the fruits of holiness." By nature we are the barren wife *and* the dead husband of Deuteronomy 25; we are totally unable to redeem ourselves.[6] In His incarnation Christ became our closest kin, taking on our nature to marry us (Eph. 5:32) and preserve our life. In heaven God's people will be married to the most faithful, beautiful, and caring spouse of all, the Lord Jesus Christ (Rev. 19:7–10).

## The Greatest Commandment (12:28–44)

Before Jesus left the temple (Mark 13:1) His enemies tested Him one more time (Matt. 22:34–35). They dared Jesus to comment on life's priorities: "Which is the first commandment of all?" In repeating the Old Testament order of love for God followed by love for one's neighbor, Jesus teaches two principles regarding religious priorities.

*Prioritizing Priorities (12:28–34, 41–44)*

First, Jesus demonstrated that love is better than religious observance (v. 33). The offerings and sacrifices in the Old Testament were symbolic of Christ's sacrifice. But they were also a tangible and costly expression of worship; God expected the best of one's possession. Still, love gives value to sacrifice (cf. 1 Cor. 13:3). It is possible to make *great* religious sacrifices without love. The Jews had become lost in a labyrinth of sacrificial duty minus sincere devotion. But in those in whom God has poured His own love, true devotion flows from the inside out (cf. Gen. 29:20).

Second, devotion to God takes priority over devotion to others. It is possible to become so frazzled taking care of others that we don't spend time in fellowship with the Lord. We will run ourselves dry if we aren't being filled up with fresh life from the Lord. To get our priorities in order we need to commune with God devotionally, not merely cerebrally. Read the Bible as God's personal expression of love toward repentant sinners. Pray to Him with sincerity, as one friend to another (John 15:13–15). Tell Him why you appreciate Him, how you have fallen short, why you are thankful, and what you need. This is what makes the gospel so powerful: When we love God (because He loved us first), He pours His love into, and out of, our hearts (Rom. 5:5).

In the light of these principles of priority Jesus said to this theological expert, "You are not far from the kingdom of God" (v. 34). The expert had an idea of what true religion is all about. But as they say, "Close enough is not good enough."

*The Missing Link (12:35–44)*

This scribe had not yet entered the kingdom of God because he was a moralist, not a Christian. He hadn't yet embraced Jesus Christ as Lord. In his close-but-lost state, he was not alone.

Jesus appealed to Psalm 110:1 to correct a pervasive mistaken notion about the Messiah. Jesus "is conversing with these men publicly for the very last time, and therefore asks the most important question of all."[7] Who is the Messiah? The Messiah is a Son of David (2 Sam. 7:12–17; Ps. 89:3–4, 34–37; Matt. 1:20; Mark 10:47–48) and the Son of God, David's Lord (Acts 2:29–31). He could be both only if He existed before and after David as the everlasting second person of the Trinity who was "conceived by the Holy Spirit and born of the Virgin Mary."[8]

Clearly, being close to the kingdom of God does not result in a changed life. Jesus warned against several faults of the scribes to which we are not immune. The scribes demanded attention by their long robes and lengthy prayers.[9] They reserved for themselves the best seats at meetings (cf. James 2:2–3) and required recognition by special greetings in the marketplaces. Worst of all, the scribes took advantage of their religious position by "devouring widows' houses" (v. 40). By contrast, Jesus used a poor widow to illustrate genuine, sacrificial, godly living (vv. 41–44). She prioritized the first commandment of the law without neglecting the second.

So many people are not far from the kingdom of God. They are like the common people of Jesus' day who "heard him gladly" (Mark 12:37). Ezekiel's sermons were similarly well-received by those who had no intention of putting them into practice (Ezek. 32:32–33). God's words to them are ominous: When judgment comes they will know that a prophet has been among them. Close enough is not good enough. It is possible to within an inch of heaven and spend an eternity in hell.

Jesus turned each of His enemies' questions into an apologetic opportunity. We need to learn how to do this so that we can always be ready to explain our hope in Christ (1 Peter 3:15). Some of our friends and neighbors might be not far from the kingdom of God. Far be it from us to not speak a word to those who are close to entering.

Jesus' enemies put Him to the test. They should have tested themselves. Test yourself in the light of Christ's law. Even those who imperfectly love God and their neighbor can still enter into the kingdom of heaven on the merits of David's Son and Lord, Jesus Christ.

## Questions

1. Why is it important to be firmly convinced of the biblical answer to the question posed in Mark 11:28?

2. How is Jesus' custom of prefacing constructive criticism with appropriate praise (cf. Rev. 2:2–4) different from what is recorded in Mark 12:14?

3. How does Romans 14:11 comment on the Herodians' flattering words in Mark 12:14?

4. How is Jesus' omniscience (cf. Mark 12:15) both comforting and terrifying?

5. How might the kinsman redeemer principle help encourage a positive view of childbearing in a culture often hostile to babies?

6. How should Mark 12:24–27 and 1 Corinthians 7:1–8 counsel a couple that is considering marriage?

7. Jesus made a solid argument for the resurrection from the Old Testament. How might He also have used Psalm 16:9–11 and Daniel 12:2?

8. Reflect on how believers today might be guilty of Jesus' accusations in Mark 12:38–40.

1. According to the Bible and under Roman law, the Jews could carry out executions themselves. But their own tradition forbade them from performing an execution during a feast. So, still fearing the people, they hoped to force Pilate to do their dirty work, avoiding the political fallout. Cf. Jakob Van Bruggen, *Christ on Earth: The Gospel Narratives as History* (Grand Rapids: Baker Books, 1998), 247–49.

2. John Calvin, *Commentary on a Harmony of the Evangelists, Matthew, Mark, and Luke* (Grand Rapids: Baker Book House, 1989), 3:45. Augustine explains that believers under the rule of the apostate and wicked emperor Julian "drew a distinction between their eternal master and their temporal master; and yet were submissive to their temporal master for their eternal master's sake." Augustine, *Expositions of the Psalms,* vol. 6 (Hyde Park, NY: New City Press, 2004), 64.

3. *Belgic Confession,* Article 7 (cf. 2 Peter 1:3).

4. In heaven redeemed saints will be like the angels, in which, ironically, the Sadducees also disbelieved (cf. Acts 23:6–9).

5. Matthew Henry, commenting on Luke 20:34–36.

6. Thomas Boston, *A View of the Covenant of Grace* (Choteau, MT: Old Path Gospel Press, 1990), 41.

7. William Hendriksen, *Exposition of the Gospel According to Mark,* New Testament Commentary (Grand Rapids: Baker, 1976), 499.

8. Apostles' Creed. Cf. Sinclair Ferguson, *Let's Study Mark* (Carlisle, PA: Banner of Truth Trust, 2002), 204.

9. Jesus is not condemning long prayers per se but showy prayers. Long, truly pious prayers are recorded in the Bible (e.g., Solomon's in 1 Kings 8:22–53). Many of the psalms are long prayers.

# TEMPLE TEACHING (2): THE END TIMES

**Mark 13:1–37**

The highest concentration of red ink in Mark's Gospel is found in the thirteenth chapter. This is the last of Jesus' speeches that Mark records before the Shepherd was struck and the sheep scattered (Mark 14:27). So what topic is important enough to warrant this much attention at this critical point in Jesus' ministry? Ironically, it is one of Christianity's most contentious subjects, the end times.

It makes sense that end-times studies can evoke strong emotions and even disagreements in the church. Christians, unlike non-Christians, place more hope in the coming age than in the present. So it's not surprising that Christians take their end-times views seriously. Still, some traditions have made their peculiar view of the end times the defining factor of their theology. When this happens, that particular view is defended vehemently and often ungraciously. Such an approach overlooks the difficulties presented by eschatology, or the study of the end times. The symbols used are often hard to interpret. Jesus Himself admits that the end times are mysterious, at least regarding the day and the hour (13:32). Much can be said about the end times, but not without caution and charity.

## Method of Interpretation

Mark 13 has been interpreted in three main ways. The first view, called the preterist view, holds that all (or at least most) of Jesus' predictions in Mark 13 have been fulfilled, largely in connection with the destruction of the temple at Jerusalem in AD 70. In the extreme, this view teaches that even the physical second coming of Christ and the final judgment have already been accomplished. Preterists argue that when Jesus insisted that "this generation will by no means pass away till all these things have taken place" (v. 30) the crises in AD 70 provide the only explanation. In response it has been argued convincingly that "this generation" "refers to the rebellious, apostate, unbelieving Jewish people," living in the past, present, and future.[1] It is also difficult to see how all of the events described in this chapter can have been fulfilled already. We are convinced that the Son of Man has not yet returned in the clouds and in great power and glory and that the elect have not yet been gathered from the earth (v. 27).

The second view, called the futurist view, teaches that all (or at least most) of Jesus' predictions in Mark 13 have yet to be fulfilled. But if Jesus is only speaking about the end of this present age then He doesn't answer the disciples' question: "Tell us when the temple will be destroyed" (v. 4; cf. v. 2). If Jesus' words are only about the end times then He failed to speak to the pressing needs of believers who were about to undergo severe persecution. In fact, Jesus does give real instructions to Jewish Christians to help them respond to the coming Roman invasion (vv. 14b–17).

A third view recognizes that in His sermon Jesus addresses events which would be fulfilled both in the near and distant future. To appreciate this view, we need to understand what question, or questions, Jesus was answering. According to Mark, Jesus began this discussion by alluding to the destruction of the temple (13:2). The disciples then asked Him when this would take place (v. 4). If only Mark were consulted, Jesus' answer would seem to be only about that single event. According to Matthew, however, the disciples also asked about "the sign of [Jesus'] coming and of the end of the age" (Matt. 24:3). In His Olivet Discourse, therefore, Jesus is answering several questions, only one of which is recorded by Mark. Jesus' speech pertains to events that are now past (connected with the destruction of Jerusalem) and still future (connected with end of the age). Obviously, from the perspective of the disciples all the events were futuristic. Also from their skewed perspective Jerusalem's fall was seen as coterminous with Christ's return and the end of the world.

Jesus corrected this mistaken notion while at the same time relating the two important events. Jerusalem's destruction both culminates in the "beginning of sorrows" (13:8) and symbolizes the end of all things. In speaking prophecy with multiple fulfillments Jesus is following the well-established Old Testament pattern.[2] It is as if Jesus is describing a distant mountain range. There is one large mountain directly in front of Him. But there are several others that extend beyond. The entire range is in focus. Jesus begins describing what is in His immediate view (the destruction of Jerusalem) but concludes with the view at the end of the horizon (His second coming and the last day). The events, though quite distinct chronologically, are spoken of as if they were close together. It is not always easy to tell where the one ends and the other begins. This method is known as "prophetic foreshortening."[3]

Consistent with the principles governing the interpretation of prophecy we will not focus on the minute particulars of Jesus' predictions. Instead we will "aim to discover the fundamental idea expressed."[4] This goal well reflects Jesus' concluding words of application (13:28–37). He gives this historical preview not to promote speculation on the identification of particular signs or to guesses about the dates of Christ's return but to promote preparedness (v. 23).

## Unpacking the Multiple Fulfillments

Understanding Jesus' use of prophetic foreshortening helps us unpack the two layers of His prophecy. The two points of Jesus' sermon could be identified as first, "The Beginnings of Sorrows," and second, "The End of the Age."

*Imminent Fulfillment: The Beginnings of Sorrows*

Beginning in Mark 13:5, Jesus answered His disciples' question relating to His prophecy that the temple would be destroyed. "Tell us, when will these things be?" they ask. "And what will be the sign when all these things will be fulfilled?" Jesus explained that there will be signs (vv. 5–8) that do not signal the end of all things (v. 7b). The beginnings of sorrow will be characterized by wars and rumors of wars (v. 7), the proliferation of deceptive false christs (vv. 5–6), and religious persecution (vv. 9–13). Throughout the book of Acts, James, Peter, Stephen, Paul, and others suffer for their faith and give their testimony before rulers and ordinary people alike. Jesus' death just a few days hence would serve as a harbinger of this persecution.

In Mark 13:8 the signs that Jesus had been describing are called "the beginnings of sorrows" or literally, "the beginning of the birth pains." Significantly, Paul uses the same word and concept to describe the great day of judgment in 1 Thessalonians 5:3. Sudden destruction will come upon those who are not prepared, "as labor pains upon a pregnant woman. And they shall not escape." What Jesus calls "the beginnings of sorrows" seems to describe events that would be fulfilled in the immediate future from the perspective of the disciples. The beginning of labor doesn't tell when the delivery will occur, but it does prove that it is coming.

The beginnings of sorrows would culminate in the Roman invasion of AD 70 (13:14–20). It is estimated that under Emperor Titus more than a million Jews, who had crowded into the city against Jesus' warning, were slaughtered. The soldiers lit fire to the temple complex and while it burned massacred children and old people, laity and priests alike. The streets ran with blood. Not surprisingly, many believers escaped because of Jesus' warning.

*Final Fulfillment: The End of the Age*
Jesus used this series of historical events that would soon take place as an illustration helping to answer the disciples' other question, "What will be the sign of Your coming and the end of the age?" (Matt. 24:3).

The end of all things will be preceded by two primary signs: gospel proclamation and religious persecution. Jesus would shortly commission His disciples to bring the gospel to all nations amid great persecution (Acts 14:22). By the end of Acts, less than a decade before Jerusalem's devastation Paul is preaching the gospel under the nose of Nero, as it were, in the heart of the most powerful empire the world has known. The gospel had made inroads into Caesar's household (Phil. 4:22). On a grander scale, before Christ returns to judge the earth the gospel will truly be communicated to the "uttermost part of the earth" (Acts 1:8, KJV). There will be disciples in all nations (Matt. 28:19).

At the last day, amid disturbances in the heavens (Mark 13:24–25; cf. 2 Peter 3:10), Christ will come and gather the elect. The Scripture gives no indication that the rapture will be secret; instead, it will be preceded by public, visible signs (cf. 1 Thess. 4:16–17). The fact that Christ's sermon culminates in a vivid description of the coming of the Son of Man (Mark 13:24–37) underscores the decisiveness of this event. All of history is careening toward the return of the great King.

## How, Then, Should We Live?

Jesus' last sermon in Mark is infused with application, largely revolving around the word *watch*. Seven times, Mark uses two different Greek words that mean "watch out," "beware," or "take heed" (13:5, 9, 23, 33, 34, 35, 37). To top off His prophetic message Jesus tells two parables with the same meaning, "Watch out!" (vv. 28–39, 34–36). Contrary to the view among some in the first-century Thessalonian church, Christ's command to watch does not condone a speculative or impractical searching of the signs (2 Thess. 3:12). Without question, watchfulness requires the active pursuit of godliness. Believers must watch their life so they will be ready to meet Christ when He calls (cf. 1 Cor. 16:13). Every Christian has a place and a task in God's kingdom. Everyone must do his part to prepare, not only himself, but others (1 Thess. 5:11) for Christ's return. But, what does this look like?

*Remember the Terror of God's Judgment (13:24)*

Judgment and hell are two scorned bywords in our day. Today it is considered uncouth to use the fear of hell as motivation to trust in Christ. "People have heard enough about hell and judgment," they say. "We need to proclaim grace and acceptance." But according to Christ those two approaches are not mutually exclusive. Christ graciously warns His friends of the coming Roman invasion.

As terrible as it was, Rome's judgment on Jerusalem would serve as a faint shadow of what the judgment of God will do to those who have not sought His favor through repentance and faith. The Bible uses revolting images of judgment to awaken sinners from their carelessness.

Even believers must never purge from their thoughts the fearful concept of hell. Cognizance of God's judgment against unrepentant sinners should always paint the backdrop of Christian gratitude (Rom. 9:22–23).

*Study Christ Diligently (13:5–6, 13)*

One of the signs of the end will be a flurry of counterfeit

christs. The best way avoid being taken by a counterfeit is to study the genuine article. Knowing the Son of God more closely keeps us from "remaining children, tossed to and fro and carried about with every wind of doctrine, by the trickery of men, in the cunning craftiness of deceitful plotting" (Eph. 4:14). It is not enough to simply confess Christ at one point in your life; you must endure to the end (Mark 3:13), growing in His grace and knowledge (2 Peter 3:18). It is impossible for the elect to be deceived (Mark 13:22). But believers are to make their "call and election sure" by exercising their knowledge of Christ through the practice of virtue, self-control, perseverance, godliness, brotherly kindness, and love (2 Peter 1:5–11). The never-passing words of Christ (Mark 13:31) radiate light on His goodness and grace for our comfort and godliness.

*Fulfill Your Evangelistic Calling (13:10)*

Like good watchmen (cf. Ezek. 33:1–11), God's people must publicize the warning that Jesus entrusts to us. The gospel *must* be preached to all nations. While the Great Commission was given the church to discharge formally through preaching and administering the sacraments (cf. Mark 16:15–16), every kingdom citizen bears responsibility for "telling the good news about the Lord Jesus" (Acts 11:20). Jesus exhorted the disciples to be prepared to speak the good news in the face of opposition. His promise to give His disciples words to say does not relieve them of their duty to prepare but assures them that, despite their own weaknesses, God will be their strength.

One serious problem that confronts the church in the face of its evangelistic imperative is the inability of many believers to articulate the gospel when the opportunity arises. Will Metzger has helpfully pointed out that the gospel message is essentially a word about God and His holiness, man and his sinfulness, Christ and His mercy, and a response of faith.[5]

*Expect Tribulation (13:8–13)*

One common theme of end-times sermons today is the claim that Christians will be raptured out of this world before the great tribulation. But such a claim seems to be patently out of step with Mark 13:24–27. It is "after the tribulation" (v. 24) that Christ's gathers "together his elect from the four winds" (v. 27). God's people have always expected tribulation. The writer to the Hebrews says that time would fail him to tell of the myriad saints who were tortured, stoned, sawn in two, slain with the sword, impoverished, afflicted, and tormented, who endured mockings, scourgings, chains, and imprisonment, "of whom the world was not worthy" (Heb. 11:32–38). Speaking from experience Paul points out that their situation wasn't unique. "All who desire to live godly in Christ Jesus will suffer persecution" (2 Tim. 3:12). The doctrine of the pre-tribulation rapture seems to undermine what Peter says in his second epistle: "Beloved, do not think it strange concerning the fiery trial which is to try you, as though some strange thing happened to you; but rejoice to the extent that you partake of Christ's sufferings, that when His glory is revealed, you may also be glad with exceeding joy" (2 Peter 2:12–13).

The overall message of Jesus' sermon is that believers should be encouraged because Christ is returning. Our hope is not in earthly success or living a good life but in seeing Christ face to face. Christ began His talk, and flustered His disciples, by saying that the earthly temple would be destroyed. Before long the disciples would realize that this temple would be replaced by one much more glorious; Christ Himself (John 2:21).

## Questions

1. What can we learn from the disciples' undue awe of the temple suggested by Mark 13:1?
2. What makes false christs so deceptive (Mark 13:5–6)?
3. How are Jesus' words in Mark 13:11 an encouragement to ordinary believers?
4. How should Mark 13:13 confront us when we attempt to win the world's love?
5. Reflect on the simplicity of the Nicene Creed's assertion that Christ "shall come again, with glory" (cf. Mark 13:26).
6. How does Mark 13:27 comfort you?
7. Some people would argue that even failed predictions of the coming of Christ are valuable because they promote thoughtfulness about the end times. Do you agree?
8. What single word could summarize Mark 13 (cf. Mark 13:37)? Meditate on this word.

1. Anthony Hoekema, *The Bible and the Future* (Grand Rapids: Eerdmans, 1979), 117. Cf. William Hendriksen, *Exposition of the Gospel According to Mark*, New Testament Commentary (Grand Rapids: Baker, 1976), 540.

2. Louis Berkhof, *Principles of Biblical Interpretation* (Grand Rapids: Baker, 1950), 153.

3. Hoekema, *The Bible and the Future*, 148.

4. Berkhof, *Principles of Biblical Interpretation*, 152–53.

5. Will Metzger, *Tell the Truth: The Whole Gospel to the Whole Person by Whole People* (Downers Grove, IL: InterVarsity Press, 1984), 44–72.

# PREPARATION FOR DEATH

---

**Mark 14:1–52**

Perhaps you've received news that was so bad—the death of a friend, the loss of a job, the disruption of a relationship—that it took some time for the news to sink completely into your psyche. Sometimes our minds need time to process the implications of major life changes. Throughout Mark's Gospel Jesus increasingly explained that He came to earth to die for His people. But not until Mark 14 does the imminence of Jesus' death finally begin to register in the disciples' hearts and minds.

Mark 11–13 describes Jesus' entry into and teaching in the temple. Jesus' end-times sermon is His last major public speech. In Mark 14 the cross approaches more rapidly than ever. The Jews secretly plot to destroy Him, His body is anointed for burial, Judas agrees to betray Him, Jesus symbolically offers His broken body and shed blood to His disciples in the Lord's Supper, and He is handed over to His killers.

Jesus is preparing Himself and His disciples for His death.

## Preliminary Preparations (14:1–11)

*Conspiracy and Betrayal (14:1, 2, 10, 11)*

In the middle of Holy Week, two days before the Passover and Feast of Unleavened Bread, the Jewish leaders "assembled at the palace of the high priest" (Matt. 26:3) to discuss how they might kill Jesus "by trickery" (Mark 14:1).[1] This conspiracy accents Jesus' holiness. There was no legal, ethical way to bring Him into judgment. Instead the high priest would illegally sacrifice Jesus for the sake of the people (cf. John 11:49–52) after the festival. Fearing that a public arrest could spark a riot (Mark 14:2), the Jews needed a spy who could signal an opportune time to apprehend Jesus "in the absence of the people" (Luke 22:6). Despite the Jews' planning, God determined that His Son would die at the hands of a wicked Jewish high priest on a public stage (Acts 26:26) on one of the busiest day of the Jewish year! "The Lord brings the counsel of the nations to nothing. . . . The counsel of the Lord stands forever" (Ps. 33:10–11)! In the words of the Latin poet and bishop Fortunatus, "Man's work faileth, Christ's availeth."[2]

Judas Iscariot, into whose heart Satan had already entered (Luke 22:3), had always followed Jesus for personal gain (John 12:6; cf. 1 Tim. 6:10). Betraying Jesus would be his last chance to profit from the man he considered to be a failed revolutionary. For his treachery, Judas received thirty pieces of silver, a guilty conscience, and—for his unrepentance—an eternity in hell. Judas and the Jewish leaders are a sobering warning to "kiss the Son, lest He be angry, and you perish in the way, when His wrath is kindled but a little" (Ps. 2:12).

In the face of this treachery we witness one of the most beautiful acts of devotion recorded in the Bible.

### Anointing (14:3–9)

Although Mark was a careful historian he intentionally broke from his commitment to chronological order when he showcases Mary's deed of devotion between two acts of treachery.[3] The Jews and Judas have plotted His death. But days earlier Jesus had already allowed Mary to anoint Him for His burial. Mark teaches us that Christ willingly went to the cross. Also, by moving Jesus' anointing closer to His death and burial, Mary's actions seem all the more fitting.

Jesus and the disciples were reclining at the table in the house of Simon the leper. In attendance at the dinner were Lazarus and his sisters Mary and Martha; Martha was serving (John 12:2). Excusing herself from the meal Mary returned with a stone jar containing a perfume extracted from a Himalayan plant. It was expensive, worth more than a year's wages. Mary broke the seal and poured the perfume over Jesus' head, rubbing it on His feet with her hair (John 12:3), anointing Him for His burial (Mark 14:8). While John uses Mary's name, Matthew and Mark simply call her "a woman," perhaps to emphasize not her personal identity but her gender. Allegations that the Bible is misogynistic are unmistakably false. In an age dominated by men, Christ and the Gospel writers consistently exalt women. Here, only a woman grasped Christ's imminent death. Misunderstanding her devotion twelve angry men grumble about her "wasteful actions." With words gushing from wells of envy, ignorance, and self-interest the disciples demonstrate the kind of hasty speech to which we can too often relate (Mark 14:5).

In response to the disciples' criticism and with the weight of the world on His shoulders, Jesus defended Mary's devotion. Jesus' disciples have allowed good things, such as social justice (Mark 14:5), to complete with worship. A dozen poor people might have been fed for a year with the money Mary spent on her perfume. But in Jesus' economy social justice can never eclipse worship. Eradication of poverty is a noble effort but not the greatest good. The good news is not that religion brings physical relief but that Christ died for sinners. Because the only lasting legacy we can leave is spiritual all our stewardship must be gospel-centered (Luke 16:9–12).

Mary understood that at the gospel's heart is Christ's death, so she presented this gospel with astounding beauty (Mark

14:6, 9). If we present the gospel in a stale, bland, or bare way, we have perverted it.

## From Passover to Lord's Supper (14:12–26)

On the night in which He was betrayed, Jesus tangibly linked one of the most solemn elements of the Jewish religion to His coming death.

*The Last Passover (14:12–21)*

In Exodus 12 God instituted the Passover as a lasting ordinance (Lev. 23:5; Num. 9:2). The substance of the ordinance consisted of eating the roasted meat of a sacrificed lamb to commemorate the sacrifice by which God's people were spared from the angel of death in Egypt. The lamb was to be eaten with unleavened bread to recall Israel's hasty exit from Egypt (Exod. 12:34), and bitter herbs to recall their suffering (v. 8). The Passover was a solemn, covenantal, or family, meal. Those outside of the covenant community could participate in the Passover meal only after joining God's people through circumcision (vv. 42–43, 48).

Jesus charged Peter and John to prepare for the Passover celebration of His small family of disciples (Luke 22:8). First, they had to find a location. Toward this end, Jesus gave rather mysterious instructions which would lead them to a house probably owned by other believers (Mark 14:13–15). Perhaps His furtiveness was to prevent Judas from knowing the location ahead of time and alerting the authorities. To this house the disciples took their lamb, killed earlier in the temple, roasted it, and prepared the remaining accouterment.[4]

The meal was progressing along the lines of Exodus 12 until Jesus dropped a bombshell: "One of you will betray Me!" The disciples were shocked. Each, filled with sorrow, began to ask, "Is it I?" With the disciples we should ask, "Who was the guilty? Who brought this upon thee? Alas, my treason, Jesus hath undone thee! 'Twas I, Lord Jesus, I it was denied thee; I crucified thee."[5] Jesus would be betrayed by a friend who dipped bread with Him in the dish (Mark 14:20; cf. Ps. 41:9). There is nothing more reprehensible in Eastern culture than to injure a host, and the Passover meal was the most intimate meal of the Jewish year. Having revealed the betrayer Jesus dismissed Judas from their midst (cf. John 13:23–26) and pronounced a curse on him (Mark 14:21). What a dreadful thing to know Jesus but still come under His curse for failing to repent.

## The Lord's Supper (14:22–26)

In instituting the Lord's Supper Jesus made plain that the thousand-year-old Passover was fulfilled in Him. The roasted lamb and the bitter herbs disappear from the supper; Christ would fill up the shed blood and bitter suffering which they designated. Instead, He used the most basic elements of a meal, bread and wine.[6] But the bread no longer represents the Israelites' hasty exit from Egypt but the body of Christ (v. 22). Christ's broken body is our deliverance from bondage to our own sinful flesh. While the disciples were drinking the wine Jesus said, "This is My blood of the new covenant, which is shed for many" (v. 24). What a shocking statement to the ears of Jewish believers whom God had told not to drink blood because of the life therein (Lev. 17:11)!

The Lord's Supper strengthens our faith by combining a physical exercise with a spiritual promise about Jesus' body and blood. These actions and words proclaim the gospel. Like the Passover, the Lord's Supper communicates our deliverance from both human bondage and divine judgment (Exod. 12:27). We receive nothing magical from the bread or wine. But we receive Christ spiritually as the elements communicate Him to us. Christ is not to be simply studied, admired, or imitated. We must feast on Him by faith, believing that in Him we have everything we need for body and soul. The Lord's Supper helps us to do that.

Like the first Passover the Lord's Supper is both a solemn remembrance and a joyful anticipation. This would be Jesus' last earthly Passover (14:25). But He would drink the fruit of the vine again in the fully realized kingdom of God. There will be a joyous marriage feast in heaven. If you are entrusting yourself to Christ you will sit at a table and drink the new wine[7] of heaven with Him.

After dinner Christ and His disciples left the warm, familiar confines of the upper room and approached the garden where He would be betrayed. Fittingly, the hymn they sang was likely a portion of Psalm 118 which extols the faithfulness of God in the face of tribulation and urges trust in God as a remedy to fear.

## Prayer and Betrayal (14:27–52)

In the cool evening air on the Mount of Olives three events took place that underscore Jesus' sacrificial service.

*A Sad Prediction (14:27–31)*

As the hour of his betrayal approached Jesus gently told His disciples that they would all stumble, literally "be scandalized," because of Him (v. 27). God would strike the Shepherd and the sheep would be scattered (Zech.13:7; cf. John 6:61, 68–69). Christ's arrest, trial, crucifixion, and death, though part of God's plan, are scandalous events which understandably rattled the disciples' faith. The Gospels reveal an ebb and flow in terms of the visibility of Christ's humanity and divinity. In Gethsemane His divinity was heavily cloaked.

Jesus singled out Peter as one who would deny Him three times (14:30). In response to Jesus' strong language ("assuredly I say to you") and specific sign ("before the rooster crows twice") stubborn, self-confident Peter insists, "I will never deny you!" Like Peter, we are often shaped by our own impressions of ourselves rather than by what God says about us. We say we are ugly; God says we are "fearfully and wonderfully made" (Ps. 139:14). We say we are sturdy; God says, "Man is like a breath" (Ps. 144:4). God's word is a true mirror, flattering or not.

Peter's shameful rant also shows us that success against sin does not come by trying harder. Peter flexed the muscles of his own resolve . . . and fell flat on his face. A short time later Jesus unveiled our greatest defense against sin: "Watch and pray, lest you enter into temptation" (14:38). Simply pledging to try harder will not make us like Jesus. But Jesus also provided a glimpse of hope. He pledged that after the disciples would abandon Him, after His resurrection He would find them in Galilee (v. 28). The good news of the gospel is rooted in the unrelenting pursuit of a loving and powerful God.

### Powerful Prayer (14:32–42)

As the night became palpable in Gethsemane Christ experienced intense isolation. Many had left Him (John 6:66), Judas had agreed to betray Him, the disciples would abandon Him and already were unable uphold Him up in prayer. He was sorrowful (even to death), troubled (Matt. 26:37–38), and distressed (Mark 14:33). The overwhelming terror of the thought of God's judgment and the weight of our sins pressed out of Him bloody sweat. The pictures of Christ praying in a composed posture serenely looking up to heaven distort reality. In Gethsemane Christ lost His composure, throwing Himself on the ground in earnest prayer (v. 35). Still, Jesus is both submissive to His Father (v. 36) and tender toward His disciples. He acknowledged their desire to stay awake and their sorrowful struggle with sleep (Luke 22:45). Mark emphasizes not the disciples' failure but the fact that Jesus alone wrestled with His accursedness. Gethsemane is a window into the infinite loneliness of hell. To God's praise, Christ's isolation secures fellowship with God.

After three bouts of prayer, Jesus received angelic aid (Luke 22:43) and returned to His disciples, calling them to march forward to meet His betrayer (Mark 14:42).

What resolve!

### Betrayal and Arrest (14:43–52)

In the dark of the garden Judas and a great multitude of soldiers face down Jesus and His disciples. Cued by Judas' betraying kiss, "They laid their hands on Him and took Him" (v. 46). Christ's words from Mark 10:33 are beginning to be fulfilled: "Behold, we are going up to Jerusalem, and the Son of Man will be betrayed to the chief priests and to the scribes." Christ's humiliation is beginning to climax. Wicked men handle Him like a criminal, though as Jesus points out, as a public figure He had never been a security threat. Now they accost Him as if He were a terrorist. They understand His threat to their godless self-interest.

Still oblivious to Christ's plan, Peter (John 18:10) tried to fulfill his vow with violence (Mark 14:47). Hear the divine resolve in Jesus' rebuke: "Do you think that I cannot appeal to My Father, and He will at once send Me more than twelve legions of angels? But how then should the scriptures be fulfilled, that it must be so?" (Matt. 26:53–54). Instead of the legions of angels Jesus chose a legion of soldiers. Those who swore never to forsake Jesus began to disappear one by one. Mark himself, who had quickly wrapped himself in a sheet after having been awakened by the news of Jesus' arrest, fled from the site, leaving the sheet behind (Mark 14:51–52). Jesus is abandoned!

Mark 14 shows that in the face of the total depravity of the Jewish leaders, in the face of the devastating breakdown of commitment by His disciples, in the face of His own overwhelmed soul, Jesus stood firm to purchase the salvation of God's people. *That* is our confidence.

## Questions

1. How does Mary's act of devotion in Mark 14:3–5 speak to those who might be marginalized by society?
2. When was the last time your devotion to Christ made you stand out?
3. How should Mark 14:7 (and Acts 20:32–35, etc.) drive us to do good to the poor?
4. How does Exodus 12:43–49 encourage us to "fence the communion table"?
5. How do these verses help us to see the Lord's Supper as an invitation to church membership?
6. How does Mark 14:19 help us to not be so confident in our works that we cease to reflect on our sin and seek the Savior's forgiveness and help?
7. How does Jesus' prayer in the garden teach us that our prayers should balance our feelings with resignation to God's will?
8. In what ways can you see yourself in Mark 14:47?

1. The Passover lamb was killed and the meal eaten on the fourteenth day of the month Nisan, on the Jewish calendar. The fifteenth day of the month marked the beginning of the seven-day Feast of Unleavened Bread. Because these holy days are so close in proximity they are often spoken of as the same event (as they are here).

2. *Psalter Hymnal* (Grand Rapids: Publication Committee of the Christian Reformed Church, 1959), song number 361.

3. Most scholars agree that the anointing took place the day before Jesus' triumphal entry (John 12:1, 12). Chronologically Jesus' anointing belongs at the end of Mark 10.

4. Unlike DaVinci's arrangement in *The Last Supper*, the disciples did not sit at chairs on one side of a tall table. Instead they reclined on pillows around a low table, each resting on his left hand, so as to leave the right free. Alfred Edersheim, *The Life and Times of Jesus the Messiah*, vol. 2 (London: Longmans, Green, 1900), 492.

5. *Psalter Hymnal*, song number 351.

6. The fact that we associate the use of wine at the Passover is due to rabbinical additions. Still, it is worth noting that when Jesus celebrated the Passover he too employed the use of wine. The Jerusalem Talmud (Pesachim 10:1) suggests that the four cups stand for the four words used in Exodus 6:6–7.

7. Interestingly, his first miracle was turning water into wine. The contention that either that wine or the Passover wine was only grape juice "is not worth serious discussion." Edersheim, *Life and Times of Jesus the Messiah*, 485 n. 2.

# INTERROGATION AND TRIAL

---

**Mark 14:53–15:15**

Sometimes God uses the most unlikely of messengers to communicate His will. In Numbers 22, God even preached through the mouth of a donkey (vv. 22–35; cf. 2 Peter 2:15–16). As Jesus advanced from Gethsemane to Golgotha He was wrongly condemned three times: first by the Sanhedrin, second by His friend Peter, third by Pontius Pilate. In each of the three unjust verdicts God communicates the gospel: The guiltless Christ suffered as a substitute for those who suffer guiltily. Throughout the interrogation and trial of Christ God preaches the substitutionary atonement of Christ. Throughout this account the overwhelming evidence is that Christ was innocent. But in the end God declared Him guilty in the place of needy believers.

Jesus was arrested in the deepest part of the night in the shadowy garden of Gethsemane. From there He was led to an even darker locale—spiritually speaking—the high priest's palace.

## Interrogation in the High Priest's Courtyard (14:53–72)

These verses reveal two great ironies. First, the judge of the world humbly submitted to a gross mistrial. Second, the great friend of sinners is denied publicly by one of His best friends. As we understand these ironies, they help us better appreciate the beauty of the gospel.

*Jesus Before the Sanhedrin (14:53–65)*

Jesus' trial was conducted not by a few zealous renegades but by the representatives of the Jewish nation (v. 53). The Sanhedrin's charter called for "able men, such as fear God, men of truth, hating covetousness" (Exod. 18:21) to keep justice among the people. Disregarding their own law, which forbade nocturnal trials concerning matters of life and death,[1] the Sanhedrin met in the middle of the night; a "legitimate" trial was held "immediately in the morning" (15:1). Determined to kill Jesus the chief priests dispatched bailiffs, sought out witnesses, interrogated the accused, and rendered judgment in an illegal trial! The only witnesses of the trial were the few servants who warmed themselves by a fire. Into this circle slipped Peter hoping to remain incognito.

Unable to find corroborating negative witnesses the chief priest practically demanded Jesus to incriminate Himself (v. 60). But, because there was no legitimate charge worthy of response, Jesus (silently) invoked Proverbs 26:4. "Do not answer a fool according to his folly, lest you also be like him." Fulfilling Scripture, Jesus "opened not His mouth" (Isa. 53:7). Peter later recalled what he witnessed that night by the flickering light of the fire: "When He was reviled, He did not revile in return . . . but committed Himself to Him who judges righteously" (1 Peter 2:23). In His silence Jesus shows His sinlessness; we can only imagine what we might have said in His place.

Jesus' interrogators eventually got to the point: "Are you the Christ, the Son of the Blessed?" (v. 61). Jesus' answer is striking: "I am! And you will see the Son of Man sitting at the right hand of the Power, and coming with the clouds of heaven" (v. 62; cf. Exod. 3:14). As the faithful witness (Rev. 1:5), Jesus condemns Himself with the truth. Jesus' prophecy looks ahead to the Day of Judgment,[2] when He will be vindicated before every living soul. The Jewish leaders, like all who misjudge Jesus, will answer for their sins. The

One they misjudged will judge them. Without sincerely weighing Jesus' testimony the high priest pretentiously tore his clothes, as if he were grieving over Jesus' "blasphemous" answer. Secretly, he was overjoyed.

Jesus had foretold that "the Son of Man will be betrayed to the chief priests and to the scribes; and they will condemn Him to death and deliver Him to the Gentiles and they will mock Him, and scourge Him and spit on Him" (Mark 10:33–34; Isa. 50:6). The Sanhedrin mocked Jesus by saying, "Prophesy to us." Jesus' answer: "I AM!"

In condemning Christ the Jewish leaders rejected God's chosen King and fulfilled the message of the prophets of which they were ignorant (Acts 13:27). Tragically, they spoke also for the Jewish people. He came to His own, and His own did not receive Him (John 1:11).

### Jesus Before Peter (14:66–72)

After Jesus' arrest Peter followed at a distance. If Peter's denial is the most visible, the other disciples denied Jesus no less by their absence. At the start of Jesus' interrogation Peter had lingered outside of the courtyard. But piggybacking on the apostle John's credentials with the high priest, Peter entered the courtyard (John 18:15–16) to within eyeshot of Jesus (Luke 22:61). Failing to watch and pray, Peter adamantly denied knowing His Savior and Friend. The words of Psalm 88:18 are fulfilled: "You have caused my beloved and my friend to shun me; my companions have become darkness" (Ps. 88:18, ESV).

Understanding how Peter could have so fallen can help us to avoid his failure. Peter's *denial* began with a passivity unbecoming a disciple of Christ. Frederick Krummacher suggests Peter's denial began when he *stealthily* approached the fire to warm himself.[3] As soon as he was called to speak, he faltered, again with an unbelieving passivity: "I don't know what you are talking about" (v. 68; cf. Luke 22:60).

Peter's escape to the porch after this first question (v. 68) might remind us of how we try to avoid situations in which spiritual questions will likely come up. When asked about our church attendance we find it easier to say, "I've always gone to church" than "I go to church because I need to be fed by the gospel every week!" In his third denial Peter invoked a curse upon himself if he was lying. Ironically, the crowd accused him of being a follower of Jesus because of his accent. The louder and longer he talked the clearer it was that he was lying![4]

Peter also betrayed a tendency toward self-protection. Succumbing to fear Peter denied Christ to protect himself. While his accuser was only a servant, she was the servant of the high priest. Could she be a spy? What about those listening nearby?

Coupled with Peter's fear may have been embarrassment at his Master's apparent defeat. Peter could not yet say with Paul, "I am not ashamed of the gospel of Christ, for it is the power of God to salvation" (Rom. 1:16). Let us take heed of our passivity, desire for self-protection, and fear of embarrassment, lest we fall too (1 Cor. 10:12).

Like Peter, our best prevention against denying Christ is to know and love Him more deeply. When the rooster crowed Jesus' and Peter's eyes met (Luke 22:61). Peter realized what he had done and was convicted of his sin. Through prayer, worship, study, and meditation Jesus becomes less deniable. "To know," in the Bible, denotes intimacy. In a sense, Peter was right when he said, "I don't know the man" (Matt. 26:72, 74). Knowing Christ always strengthens us against spiritual lapses.

But what do we do when the rooster's crow reminds us that we too have denied Christ? Like Peter, we should weep over our failures and redeem available second chances. The servant girl's first accusation might have caught Peter off guard, leading him to answer in a bewildered panic. Peter probably hated what he had done, but he was too concerned about his own safety and reputation. His heart wasn't yet broken by his sin. When Peter truly reflected on his failure, he wept tears leading to repentance (2 Cor. 7:9–10). We might like to read that after Peter was convicted of his sin he rushed back to the fire to set the record straight, but this doesn't happen—until Pentecost. When we find ourselves filled with regret over wasting an opportunity to speak about Christ or over outright denying Him, we should look for opportunities for redemption.

## On Trial Before Pilate (15:1–15)

Having already found Jesus guilty during the night the Sanhedrin wasted no time in capping off their scheme by meeting "officially" first thing in the morning to announce the guilty verdict.[5] Eager to get Jesus into the hands of Pilate, the Roman executioner, they bound Him and led Him away, like an animal, like the scapegoat of Leviticus 16:20–21. Although the Jews might have immediately stoned Jesus for blasphemy, they delivered Him to the Gentiles. God was at work fulfilling the Scriptures. He must be crucified (Gal. 3:13; cf. Mark 10:33). Christ would die an accursed death on a Roman cross.

Though the regions of Samaria and Judea were relatively small holdings of the Roman Empire, as an extension of Caesar's rule, Pontius Pilate's word was law to those beneath him. Shrewdly, therefore, the Jews downplayed the charge of religious blasphemy knowing it would hold little weight in a Roman law court. Of the many charges which the Jews presented before Pilate the three that are preserved could not be ignored by a Roman administrator: perverting the nation, forbidding the payment of tribute to Caesar, and declaring Himself to be a king (23:2; cf. John 18:29–32). In short, they presented Jesus as a politically dangerous man.

Of course, the charges are as false as they were apropos. Far from perverting the nation, as the Israel of God, Christ came to restore the nation from perversion (Hos. 11:1; Matt. 2:15). Far from keeping the Jews from giving tribute to Caesar, He commanded it (Mark 12:17). And far from being a civil anarchist, Jesus faithfully submitted to the governing authorities. His kingdom, while opposed to Caesar's on many points (John 19:12), is a spiritual kingdom, not of this world (18:36). Christ never physically challenged civil authority, and Pilate knew it. But because the Jews craved Jesus' death the crime had to fit the punishment.

During the trial Jesus answered straightforward questions (14:61–62; 15:2) while at the same time refusing to refute the trumped-up charges. Jesus' silence punctuated the lies with which He was accused. In the face of Jesus' "good confession" (1 Tim. 6:13) Pilate marveled, "Why doesn't He defend Himself?" Because His goal is the cross!

Probably the chief priest could tell that Pilate had no intention to execute Jesus. In fact, he was mindful to let Him go. Enter Barabbas.

### Jesus and Barabbas

Pilate had a custom of releasing a prisoner on Passover. On this Passover he hoped to extricate himself from an awkward political–moral dilemma by delivering Jesus. In addition to freeing this just Man, Pilate hoped also please the crowd because Jesus was despised only by the envious leaders (15:10). Interestingly, as secular history demonstrates, Pilate was no friend of the Jews. He only eventually capitulated to their demands out of self-interest. To Pilate's surprise, the crowd rejected his offer to release Jesus. Only days ago the walls of Jerusalem resounded with declarations that Jesus was "the king who comes in the name of the Lord!" (Luke 19:38). But the religious leaders worked hard to stir up and persuade (Matt. 27:20) the crowd to have Pilate release for them Barabbas instead (Mark 15:11). How great is the power of envy! The leaders were so envious of Jesus that they stopped at no length to destroy Him. They even risked offending the crowd among which Jesus was still popular. To avoid strict divine judgment, leaders must be certain that they are leading with heavenly motives and not self-interest. As followers, we must be certain that we are not mindlessly following ambitious leaders. After all, despite the leadership's strong-arming, the crowd was not innocent of Jesus' death. It was they who "delivered up and denied [Jesus] in the presence of Pilate when he was determined to let Him go" (Acts 3:13).

Jesus' trial ended on an anticlimax with Pilate pronouncing a conflicting verdict (vv. 14–15). After examining the evidence (John 23:13–14) he found Jesus innocent. Still, Pilate cowardly tested the political waters. Caving to popular opinion, Pilate changed his verdict. He consulted the "opinion polls" to try to scratch the itching ears of the masses (2 Tim. 4:3). He wanted to gratify the crowd because, as a spineless, people-pleasing opportunist, ultimately he wanted to gratify himself. Partisan to his own special interests Pilate abdicated his position of moral leadership.

## Scourged for Us

Jesus endured an outrageously unjust trial to face scourging and crucifixion, two of the most gruesome forms of punishment imaginable. With a reserved reverence the Gospels simply tell us that "Pilate took Jesus and scourged Him" (John 19:1; cf. Matt. 27:26; Mark 15:15). The scourge consisted of a handle to which were connected several ropes or leather straps. Hard objects such as stone, metal, shells, or bone could be attached to the straps. Scourging was sometimes fatal. Paul, when faced with the horrific prospect of being scourged, chose to avoid this punishment by asserting his rights (Acts 22:25). Christ accepted the scourge's pain knowing that by His stripes we are healed (Isa. 53:5). Christ graphically describes part of the price of our salvation by saying "The plowers plowed on My back; they made their furrows long" (Ps. 129:3).

As Jesus' arms were bound and stretched above his head for scourging, Barabbas was released from his bonds and slipped into the crowd, free. That "notorious prisoner" (Matt. 27:16), insurrectionist, robber (John 18:40), and murderer is a dark symbol of natural man. When Barabbas was loosed as Christ was bound, God is telling us that there is hope for us (cf. Matt. 5:21–22)!

When Pilate delivered Jesus to death (vv. 1, 15) he, unknowingly, acted as God's agent (Rom. 8:32; Eph. 5:2). God used Pilate's wicked cowardice to fulfill His own predetermined purpose of saving the people whom He loved (Acts 4:27–28). Pilate's failure exalts the leadership of Christ who quietly, faithfully, lovingly does what is necessary for our salvation. Pilate pursued justice until things got uncomfortable for him. Jesus pursued justice to the very end!

Christ's ministry was characterized by the rejection and isolation which was most evident in the shadow of the cross. But all this rejection set up the climax of Christ's resurrection. In the resurrection the Father reversed the verdict of Pilate and the Sanhedrin, by declaring Jesus innocent. He reversed the verdict of Peter by confessing His Son before a stunned world. The great story of the Bible is not man's failure but God's victory. This interrogation draws our attention not to man but to the righteous and faithful God, our Lord Jesus Christ.

Living as we do, in the midst of trials and difficulties, this is exactly the message we need to hear.

## Questions

1. Do you ever feel like you are following Jesus "at a distance" (Mark 14:54)?

2. How, like Peter, might we be tempted to downplay our relationship with Christ (Mark 14:68)?

3. How can we learn from Peter's fall to follow Jesus more closely?

4. Meditate on this phrase in connection with Mark 15:1: "He was bound that we might be loosed from our sins."[6]

5. When might it be wise for us to follow Jesus' example in "answering nothing" (Mark 15:3, 5)?

6. Reflect on the dangers of asking for the opinion of others when you already know the right thing to do.

7. Reflect on the beautiful scandal of Barabbas's release as it points to our redemption.

8. How can Christ's wounds provide comfort for our physical pain?

1. Mishna, Sanhedrin IV.1. Cited in William Hendriksen, *Exposition of the Gospel According to Mark*, New Testament Commentary (Grand Rapids: Baker, 1976), 607.
2. More immediate fulfillment of Jesus' prophecy might be found in His appearances at Stephen's stoning and Paul's conversion.
3. F. W. Krummacher, *The Suffering Savior* (Chicago: Moody Press, 1947), 156.
4. Hendriksen, *Exposition of the Gospel According to Mark*, 621.
5. The word for consultation (v. 1) is always used by the Gospel writers to denote unscrupulous scheming; five times in Matthew, twice in Mark, once in Acts.
6. "Form for the Celebration of the Lord's Supper," *Psalter Hymnal* (Grand Rapids: Publication Committee of the Christian Reformed Church, 1976), 144.

# FROM THE CROSS
# TO THE GRAVE

---

**Mark 15:16–47**

For two hundred years Christians have sung, "In the cross of Christ I glory, towering o'er the wrecks of time; all the light of sacred story gathers round its head sublime."[1] Surely the story of God's redemption does gather around the cross of Christ. But as we begin to look into the events of Christ's crucifixion we wonder, "Where is the glory?" Instead we see shame, humiliation, and gloom. If the cross is glorious, its glories are veiled to natural man under a dark curtain.

## He Was Crucified (15:16–32)

Mark's crucifixion narrative describes Christ's final hours in four locations: the Praetorium, the road out of Jerusalem, Golgotha, and the cross; each one step lower in His descent into hell.

### Jesus' Suffering in the Praetorium (15:16–20)

The soldiers who led Jesus to the Praetorium (Matt. 27:27), or Roman headquarters, saw Him as just another—though notorious—"criminal" to be punished. For them Jesus could later pray, "Father forgive them, for they know not what they are doing" (Luke 23:34). They stripped Him of His clothes and, mocking His claim to royalty, wrapped Him in a scarlet robe and pressed a crown of thorns upon His head. William Hendriksen points out that every thorn prick we experience is a reminder of the curse of the ground (Gen. 3:18). Now Christ takes upon His own head this thorny curse.[2] Into His hand they put a flimsy reed to symbolize a scepter. They knelt in phony homage before Him. With His own "scepter" they struck Him on the head (Matt. 27:30). With each blow, the scepter drove the thorns deeper into Christ's brow. Finally, the soldiers refitted Jesus with His own dirty, bloody clothes.

It is amazing that we can care so much for our dignity when our Savior allowed Himself to be stripped and utterly humiliated to win our salvation! Jesus' dignity bowed before His mission.

### Jesus' Suffering on the Road out of Jerusalem (15:21)

The Old Testament required that the sin offering be made outside the camp (Exod. 29:14; Lev. 4:21) signifying sin's repulsiveness. As the great sin offering, Jesus was appropriately sacrificed outside the camp (Heb. 13:11–12). Exiting the Praetorium the soldiers hefted the heavy cross upon Jesus' lacerated back. Dragging His burden behind Him He began that painful walk to Golgotha—like a more modern criminal being forced to build his own gallows in the center of town. In fulfilling Old Testament imagery the greater Son of Promise carried His own wood to the sacrificial alter (Gen. 22:6). Because of the beating Christ had received He became unable to carry the cross. The man conscripted to carry it, Simon from Cyrene, likely later became a Christian (Rom. 16:13). As He walked great crowds of people wept over Jesus (Luke 23:27–31). Weak as He was Jesus warned them to heed instead their own future. Jesus preached the gospel to the end!

### Jesus' Suffering at Golgotha (15:22–24)

Arriving at Golgotha ("Place of a Skull") Jesus was offered myrrh-laced wine to dull the pain; perhaps an intended love token from His few lingering friends. Raising it to His lips

He discerned its character (Matt. 27:34). Because He desired a clear mind as He ministered from the cross, reciting and fulfilling Scripture, He refused to drink.[3] He manfully drank from His Father's cup to the last accursed drop, enduring the full measure of divine chastisement for our redemption.

Again, Jesus' garments were removed and divided. When Adam sinned God clothed him. When Christ atoned for our sin God stripped Him. He was stripped naked so that we would not have to appear naked before God but instead be clothed in His righteousness.

### Jesus' Suffering on the Cross (15:25–32)

At Golgotha Jesus was stretched out on the cross as soldiers drove nails into His hands and feet. As the base of the cross dropped into its hole in the ground His body rippled with pain.[4] Hung between heaven and earth, with a criminal indictment pinned above His head, Christ was counted as a transgressor (vv. 27–28; cf. Isa. 53:12).

God does not delight in the death of the wicked (Ezek. 33:11). By contrast, the Jewish leaders relished in the death of the Righteous. "Come down, and we'll believe in you!" they cried. Despite the great temptation to lash out in self-defense Christ remained on the cross. To prove His great love for us, Christ endured mocking by both great and small—including common criminals (vv. 29–32).

The design of crucifixion was to make a public spectacle of the accused. In God's providence, the real public spectacle was the "principalities and powers" that Christ defeated at the cross (Col. 2:15). "The greater . . . disgrace which He endured before the world so much the more acceptable and noble a spectacle did He exhibit in His death to God."[5] With all our hearts we can sing, "In the cross of Christ I glory, towering o'er the wrecks of time!"

## He Died (15:33–41)

As Christ suffocated on the cross, Mark's great theme verse neared fulfillment: "The Son of Man did not come to be served but to serve and to give His life a ransom for many" (10:45).

*Last Moments (15:33–36)*

From noon until three, darkness blanketed the land offering poetic commentary on the scene at Golgotha. As the plague of darkness symbolized God's judgment against Egypt (Exod. 11:21–23), so this miraculous darkness publicly denounced the treasonous actions of apostate Israel. It also symbolized the hellish judgment that was falling upon Christ. God turned the radiance of His face from Jerusalem, where the curse-bearer hung. "Hell came to Calvary that day, and the Savior descended into it and bore its horrors in our stead."[6] At the darkest hour of history God was doing a great work. Believers experience the light of God's grace because Christ experienced the darkness of dereliction. His loss is our gain.

The last words of Christ that Mark records reflect the dreadful darkness smothering the land: "God, God . . . my God! Why did you dump me miles from nowhere?" (Ps. 22:1, MSG). In His humanity and under the duress to which He had been subjected, the Son lost sight of the Father's abiding love. In the capacity of Only Begotten Son Christ is never forsaken by His Father. But as sin-bearer (2 Cor. 5:21) He is rejected so that we might never be. To His cry, Christ received no immediate answer, neither from the Father nor from Elijah.[7] For a time, the Father offered no help that He might demonstrate the gravity of the atonement.

*Last Breath (15:37)*

His last loud cry (v. 37) is evidence of both the physical and spiritual torment He endured on our behalf. When Christ realized the full weight of God's opposition to Him as sin-bearer He cried out in terror. Still, even under unspeakable torment, He died not in despair but in hope: "Father, into thy hands I commit my spirit" (Luke 23:46, KJV). Even when questioning His forsakenness He addressed the Lord as "my God." Entrusting Himself to the care of His father, He breathed His last.

The Christian's experience of death has been softened by Christ's. He died under the curse of God; we die in a perfect right standing before God. He died forsaken; we die having been accepted in the beloved (Eph. 1:6) and in fellowship with God through His Spirit. Because Christ committed His soul in death to the Lord, we can do the same. As this last breath exited Christ's body the ransom that He came to pay was paid. Herein is our hope. A day is coming when each of us will breathe our last. The only way to prepare for that day is to commit ourselves to Jesus.

### Witnesses of Christ's Death (15:38–41)

As Paul would later remind King Agrippa, Christ died not in a hidden corner but on a public stage before hosts of witnesses. According to Mark, one witness to Christ's death was the veil that separated the temple's Holy Place from the Most Holy Place (Exod. 26:33). Here, once a year, God would meet with the high priest who represented the people (Heb. 9:4). The writer to the Hebrews interprets this veil, that way into the Holy of Holies, as a symbol of Christ's flesh (Heb. 10:19–25). Christ's broken body is the new and living approach to God. During the old dispensation, any outsider who came near the veil was killed (Num. 18:17). In Christ we approach God with confidence (vv. 19, 22; Eph. 2:14).

Another witness to Christ's death was the centurion (v. 39). Something about Christ's death wrested from His own killer a surprising confession: "This man was the Son of God." "The centurion must have felt how nature reacted to the death of Jesus."[8] He might have perceived that Christ reverently wrestled with God His Father and died as a faithful Son. The Man whom he had just helped to kill was no mere man.

A third witness to Christ's death was a group of devoted women (vv. 42–43a). The world of Jesus' time viciously discriminated against women. But God honored women as witnesses of His death and resurrection; with the exception of John we know of no man who lovingly followed Jesus to the cross. So many women followed Jesus because He didn't judge them by their gender. Through their contact with the Savior they were emboldened to live vigorous Christian lives, sharing in the ministry of Christ. These women, like their male co-workers, labored in the ministry of the gospel because they looked to Jesus (v. 40) for comfort in life and in death. Those who look to Jesus find that no personal sacrifice for God is too great.

## He Was Buried (15:42–47)

All burials are solemn events. If not for the burial of Christ, they would also all be tragic. Christ's burial is the last stage of His humiliation. It is also the beginning of His glorification and the basis for any human hope beyond the grave.

### Background to the Burial (15:42-43a)

Because it was unlawful for a body to hang overnight and because that particular evening brought on the Sabbath, Jesus' body was quickly removed before dusk (Luke 23:54; cf. Deut. 21:23). For this reason a nearby grave was used (John 19:41). Jesus' body, like the bodies of all those who died an accursed death, also needed to be removed by evening to prevent the land from being defiled at the start of a new day.[9] Jesus' body was removed from the cross to signify the removal of the curse. Sin's wages have been paid. The sacrifice is now handled with honor and dignity.

The "undertaker," Joseph of Arimathea, was a good and righteous man (Luke 23:50) who was looking for the kingdom

(Mark 15:43) and had not consented to Jesus' death (Luke 23:51). It is striking that both he and his accomplice, Nicodemus, were respected members of the Sanhedrin (Mark 15:43). God's grace can win over even the most natural of enemies.

Both men were secret disciples of Jesus (John 19:38; Matt. 27:57) who "because of the Pharisees . . . did not confess Him, lest they should be put out of the synagogue; for they loved the praise of men more than the praise of God" (John 12:42). Because the entire council condemned Him to death (Mark 14:64) Joseph, an influential, good man, might have absented from the vote. As Edmund Burke said, "All that is necessary for evil to triumph is for good men to do nothing." Joseph had learned this lesson and now enlisted his influence and affluence (Matt. 27:57) in the service of God.

### Joseph's Request and Action (15:43b–47)

When Joseph asked Pilate for Jesus' body he was endangering his good position as a prominent councilman. But this secret disciple had been strengthened by the death of Christ. He now answered God's call to not waste the opportunities each of our respective prominence affords. Having received permission from Pilate, Joseph and Nicodemus proceeded to care for the body:

> Jesus' body is wrapped completely in a linen shroud . . . [with] a sweat cloth . . . wrapped around the head. Considering the large quantity of ointment (75 pounds) we have to imagine that the entire body and head were covered, with the cloths and the surrounding shroud drenched in ointment and formed, as it were, into a fragrant, protective second skin . . . Jesus' burial is lavish.[10]

The way that Joseph and Nicodemus cared for the body of Jesus contributes to a theology for the care of the dead. Christians care for bodies because God cares for bodies.

By reflecting the manner in which the Firstfruits of the resurrection was buried (1 Cor. 15:20) we give tangible credence to our belief in the resurrection. By contrast, in the Bible cremation is a sign of judgment, not honor (1 Kings 13:2). It is no wonder that Joseph did not burn Jesus' body on a pyre, collect the ashes, and store them in a jar. That Joseph buried Christ in his own tomb (v. 46) reveals that he was preparing for his own eternity even when he was completely healthy. Modern longevity may incline us to forget about the brevity of life. But the godly prepare for death without superstition.

*Why Was Christ Buried?*
Christ was buried "to prove that he really died."[11] Jesus' death was witnessed by huge crowds, demonstrated by a soldier's spear, and certified by the Roman governor. He was copiously embalmed and sealed in a tomb before eyewitnesses. Allowing, for the sake of argument, that Jesus did not rise from the dead and that the disciples really did steal Jesus' body, what they stole was a dead body (Matt. 28:13). But hundreds of witnesses saw Jesus alive over the next forty days. The burial narrative confirms Jesus' death, beyond a shadow of doubt, and sets up the marvelous resurrection account.

Still, Christ's tomb speaks to more than the reality of His death. Jesus sanctified the grave. It is unsettling to think about dying. If Christ's body had simply ascended into heaven from the cross we wouldn't know how to relate to the grave. But Christ's burial (and subsequent resurrection) teach us that death need not be damning. As the good shepherd, Christ never leads where He has not first gone Himself. Now in heaven Christ gently leads us to our own graves saying, "I've been there before and will lead you through. Trust Me."

Some time ago, someone asked me the kind of question pastors love to hear: "How can I grow in love for God?" That's a great question. The greatest commandment is not to be successful for God, or appreciated by people, but to love God. If I had to give just one answer to that question it would be this: We grow in love for God by looking to the cross (cf. 1 John 4:10). There we

> See from his head, his hands, his feet, sorrow and love flow mingled down. Did e're such love and sorrow meet? Or thorns compose so rich a crown? Were the whole realm of glory mine that were a present far too small. Love so amazing, so divine, demands my soul, my life, my all.[12]

## Questions

1. Calvin says that these verses "call for secret meditation, rather than for the ornament of words." Why is this so? If possible, spend some time meditating on these verses.
2. How can you be strengthened by the prolonged mocking which Jesus endured (cf. 1 Peter 2:23–24)?
3. How does Christ's forsakenness comfort us during our seasons of forsakenness?
4. How does Christ illustrate that death is a violent rending of body and soul (Mark 15:37)?
5. How can we commit our souls to God in life and in death?
6. Are you tempted, like Joseph and Nicodemus, to be a secret disciple? Are you willing to be known as a disciple at church but not when you are on the playground, the job site, or your computer? Whose praise is more important to you?
7. How does an honorable burial show honor both to our humanity and to our Maker?
8. List several ways in which Christ's crucifixion, death, and burial were dishonorable. Marvel at how Christ lowered Himself.

1. John Bowring, "In the Cross of Christ I Glory," *Psalter Hymnal* (Grand Rapids: Publication Committee of the Christian Reformed Church, 1976), song number 429.

2. William Hendriksen, *Exposition of the Gospel According to Mark*, New Testament Commentary (Grand Rapids: Baker, 1976), 644.

3. Later, in response to Jesus' words, "I thirst," He is given a sponge full of vinegar (Luke 19:28–29). Because this sour wine was not mingled with myrrh He felt free to drink (John 19:30).

4. Perhaps because of its gruesome nature and out of reverence to Jesus none of the Gospel writers gratuitously describe the actual crucifixion.

5. John Calvin, *Commentary on a Harmony of the Evangelists, Matthew, Mark, and Luke* (Grand Rapids: Baker Book House, 1989), vol. 1, 296.

6. Hendriksen, *Exposition of the Gospel According to Mark*, 660.

7. The onlookers mistook Christ's cry as directed to Elijah (vv. 35–36). His name in Aramaic sounds similar to the name of God that Christ used. Christ's question is answered as He is glorified beginning with His resurrection (cf. Ps. 22:21).

8. Hendriksen, *Exposition of the Gospel According to Mark*, 666. Matthew tells us (27:51–54) that other miraculous events took place which contributed to the response of faith.

9. Cf. John Calvin, *Commentaries on the Four Last Books of Moses Arranged in a Harmony* (Grand Rapids: Baker Books, 1989), vol. 3, 47–48.

10. Jakob Van Bruggen, *Christ on Earth: The Gospel Narratives as History* (Grand Rapids: Baker Books, 1998), 272.

11. *Heidelberg Catechism*, Q&A 41.

12. Isaac Watts, "When I Survey the Wondrous Cross," *Psalter Hymnal* (Grand Rapids: Publication Committee of the Christian Reformed Church, 1976), song number 350.

# FROM THE GRAVE TO THE SKY

————————▶ ● ◀————————

**Mark 16:1–20**

When was the last time your plans were frustrated? It can be discouraging when intentions don't materialize. But sometimes it's a good thing.

Three women had intended to enter Jesus' tomb and soak His body with fragrant herbs and oils. But their plans were frustrated; this was the day of Christ's resurrection!

Theirs wasn't the only plan that went afoul. When Christ rose from the grave and issued the Great Commission, He also defeated the devil's plan to crush the Son of God and the spread of His gospel.

## Jesus' Resurrection (16:1–8)

For two dark nights, Jesus' body rested in the tomb. But the time of His humiliation was nearly over.

### The Cusp of the Resurrection (16:1–3)

Mark sets the stage for Jesus' resurrection by giving two important details. The first detail has to do with the love labor of three women; an unusual emphasis considering that female testimony was not admissible in the law courts of Jesus' day. If the resurrection, the crux of Christianity, was a fabricated tale its inventors would not have been so foolish as to use female testimony. As it is, God freely exalts the status of women in this critical event.

The three women were Mary Magdalene,[1] Salome,[2] and Mary the mother of James. These women had followed Jesus for some time and supported Him by their own means (Luke 8:3). Compelled by a courageous love for Jesus, they hoped to apply additional spices and ointments to Jesus' body. Not surprisingly, their love was checked by fear as they traveled to the tomb. Their concern about moving the stone from the tomb's entrance betrays their doubts about Christ's promise to rise on the third day (Mark 10:34). Little faith sees problems where they don't exist. Indeed, the stone had already been rolled away (v. 4).

A second important detail concerns the timing of the women's approach; it was very early on the first day of the week. Christ's resurrection forever changed the Christian calendar. The highest day of the week is now the first day. In the Old Testament the pattern was work before rest (Exod. 20:11). In the New Testament, because of Christ's work, the pattern is rest before work. Therefore, we begin our week by resting in Christ that we might be strengthened to work for His glory. In submission to God's will (Isa. 58:13) and displaying a careful piety often lacking among believers today, these women bought their spices after having rested on the Sabbath (Luke 23:56). The issues pertaining to God's Holy Day are complex. Still, we should wonder if we have lost something of the reverence of these women.

*Presence of Angels (16:4–7)*
When the women arrived at the tomb they were surprised to see it open. They were still more astonished to see angels[3] before whom they bowed their faces to the ground (Luke 24:5). These hearty women weren't scared because they were girls. When the seasoned Roman guards had seen the angels—their appearance was like lightning (Matt. 28:3) and their apparel shone like the sun reflecting off fresh snow (Luke 24:4)—they had trembled and became like dead men (Matt. 28:4).

The first thing the angels did upon the arrival of the three visitors was to pronounce words of comfort: "Do not be alarmed" (v. 6). How gracious the Lord is to encourage those who fear due to little faith. Second, the angels demonstrated the reality of the resurrection by pointing to where the now-risen Christ had lain. Jesus' body rose right through the grave clothes still in plain sight (John 20:6–7). The stone was rolled away not to let Jesus out but to let witnesses in. Third, the angels give instructions for faithfulness. The women were to tell the disciples exactly what Jesus had already told them (Luke 24:6–8; Mark 14:27–28). "Tell His disciples—and Peter—that He is going before you into Galilee; there you will see Him as He said to you" (v. 7). Jesus approached the grave as a suffering Servant. He rose again as a victorious King. Yet he remains the same "thoughtful, kind, and loving Lord."[4] Jesus' reference to Peter is especially touching considering his recent lapse of faith and courage (14:66–72). Perhaps this is why Peter (with John) was the first apostle to run to the tomb (Luke 24:12; John 20:2–4).

*Pursuant Action by the Women (16:8)*

The women left the tomb amazed. The Greek word (*ekstasis*) describes the state of someone who is thrown into a state of blended fear and wonderment.[5] It is on this note of bewilderment that the book of Mark ends—at least according to many scholars, including conservative scholars. Citing both external and internal evidence, scholars contend that verses 9–20 are a later addition to the Gospel appended to tie up loose ends. In terms of external evidence, these verses are absent from several early manuscripts viewed by some as the most reliable. Concerning internal evidence, the grammar, style, and contents of the longer ending seem to some to be incongruous with the rest of the book.

In wrestling through this difficult issue we need to see this as one of the truly rare cases in which manuscript questions concern a considerable number of verses,[6] though notably, no Christian doctrine rests on these verses; nearly all the concepts are summaries of other portions of Scripture. To be brief, given that these verses have been preserved in the church's Bibles for nearly two thousand years in a preponderance of manuscripts, it seems wise for us to receive them as authoritative.

But what if verses 9–20 were not authentic? The alternate ending, verse 8, is striking. Christ's resurrection filled these women with the kind of fear that is greatly needed today. In the words of one social commentator:

> A healthy fear of God is totally lost on contemporary Christianity, which sees him as more of a "buddy/ friend/therapist/guru" than the creator and sustainer of the universe. More and more young people are growing dubious of God-lite and prefer thinking of him as a commanding, dominating, dangerous God who deserves our deferential fear.

He then adds this quote from J. I. Packer:

> The pitiable Savior and the pathetic God of modern pulpits are unknown to the old gospel. The old gospel tells men that they need God, but not that God needs them (a modern falsehood); it does not exhort them to pity Christ but announces that Christ has pitied them, though pity was the last thing they deserved. It never loses sight of the divine majesty and sovereign power of the Christ whom it proclaims but rejects flatly all representations of him that would obscure his free omnipotence.[7]

Have we lost the fear of God? Test yourself. When you think about the resurrection, do you only think about yourself and those you love who will be raised some day? Or, like these women, do you tremble in reverent admiration before the God who has soundly defeated the great enemy death, and who will similarly defeat everyone who refuses to submit to Him?

In spite of their fear, the women were not distracted from their mission. Unbelieving fear is crippling. Godly fear is energizing. One of the saddest attributes describing modern Christians is lethargy, the state of being sluggish or indifferent. Those plagued by lethargy need to go the tomb, believe that Christ is raised, tremble in amazement, and be energized for faithfulness.

## Jesus' Final Words and Deeds (16:9–20)

Following Jesus' resurrection, in obedience to His instructions (Matt. 26:32), Jesus' disciples should have proceeded immediately to Galilee. They did not. Knowing their little faith, Jesus lingered in Jerusalem for another week making a number of appearances to His frightened followers.

*Christ's Appearances (16:9–14)*

While the women prepared to leave the tomb-garden to locate the other disciples (cf. John 20:11–18) Jesus appeared first to Mary, comforting her grieving heart and steeling her to face a doubting audience (vv. 10–11). Later, Jesus appeared to two disciples who also met with disbelief upon giving their report. Like the disciples, we might resist the testimony of others because we think so highly of ourselves. How many times have we shrugged off a Christian messenger because we didn't like the message (or the messenger)? Jesus rebuked His disciples for failing to heed His heralds (v. 14). But Mark's record of the disciples' doubt also sounds a note of comfort. Doubt is not praiseworthy, but it is a reality for believers. God continually blesses us with the Word and sacraments "because of our weakness and because of our failures, in order to increase our faith by feeding us with the body and blood of Jesus Christ."[8]

As the disciples grappled with their little faith and the wonderful but fearful reality of the resurrection, Christ issued His Great Commission.

### Christ's Assignment (16:15–18)

While the disciples huddled around a table in a secret room the risen Lord entered through shut doors and gave His marching orders. It's fair to say that He had captured His disciples' attention! A healthy fear of the risen Christ is essential to a faithful response to His evangelistic imperative. If we don't fear God we will view the Great Commission merely as a good suggestion.

Jesus' commission contains two parts. The first is a commandment to preach the gospel, not morality or integrity. Our message is the offer of free grace for sinners on the basis of Christ's perfect righteousness. This gospel is a two-edged sword. He who believes, and confirms his faith with baptism, will be saved. But he who does not believe will be condemned. The eleven disciples could not possibly go into all the world and speak this message to every creature (v. 15). That's our job. There are people in your life who might never meet an ordained minister or sit under the formal preaching of God's Word. You are their evangelist.

The second part of Jesus' commission is a promise. Like Elisha receiving the mantle of Elijah (1 Kings 19:9–14), as Jesus' apostles would discharge their evangelistic duty, He would confirm His blessing through signs (vv. 17–18). While these verses probably speak to what would happen when Jesus' authority was transferred to His original disciples,[9] just as in the commission itself, God speaks here to the modern church. Faith in the gospel is self-authenticating. The remarkable fruit of faithful living will testify to God's miraculous working in believers' lives. Christ calls us to live courageously, trusting God for protection. This does not authorize us to throw caution to the wind. But it does assure us that God supports His troops.

Mark's last verses summarize Jesus' ascension and the outworking of His commission.

*Christ's Ascension (16:19–20)*
Forty days after His resurrection Christ physically departed from His disciples. Christ was received up into heaven as a visible affirmation that His redeeming work had been accomplished. Jesus passed through the heavens (Heb. 4:14) to sit at God's right hand (Heb. 9:24) to fulfill His eternal ministry of intercession for those who come to God through Him (Heb. 7:25).

But true to His promise to never forsake His disciples Christ remains spiritually. No mention of Pentecost is made in the last two verses. But Mark's claim that the previously tremulous disciples went out and preached everywhere (v. 20) can be explained only by the coming of the Holy Spirit, the other counselor whom Christ had promised (John 14:16; Acts 1:7–8). Believers today have Christ's same spiritual presence that made the disciples braver than ever.

Jesus walked this earth as one of us, having taken on a human nature; a real human body and soul. When He returned to heaven He did not shed this. The disciples saw a real person go up to heaven. What an encouragement this is for us who rightly crave remade bodies and souls. Christ ascended into heaven as a pledge that He will take us to Himself. Of this promise the Holy Spirit stands as earnest.

## Conclusion: Applying Mark's Gospel

Mark's aim was to demonstrate "the gospel of Jesus Christ, the Son of God" (Mark 1:1). The gospel is the good news that despite alienation because of our sin, we can become children of God through faith in His Son. In the "action Gospel" Mark unfolds his theme with straightforward recounting and reflection on Jesus' entire life and ministry. Jesus not only taught the gospel; He also brought it to bear in people's lives through deeds. He served His disciples. He healed the sick. He fed the hungry. He drove away the wicked and unrepentant. He bled, thirsted, and died.

John was thinking of Christ when he said, "My little children, let us not love in word or in tongue, but in deed and in truth" (1 John 3:18). Such love is always costly. Mark was a very close follower of Peter. For this reason some have called Mark's Gospel "The Gospel According to Peter." Peter said, "Beloved, do not think it strange concerning the fiery trial which is to try you, as though some strange thing happened to you; but rejoice to the extent that you partake of Christ's sufferings, that when His glory is revealed, you may also be glad with exceeding joy" (1 Peter 4:12–13). More than any other Gospel, Mark focuses on the suffering and death of Christ. This fact helps us to remember that the substitutionary atonement of Christ is the heartbeat of our religion. Our hope rests not on what we do but what Christ has done.

What He has done is described by Mark in kingdom terms. Jesus didn't come merely preaching a message of personal salvation. He came preaching a message of the kingdom. Today it's fashionable to divide spiritual matters into the categories of "salvation issues" and "non-salvation issues." But such compartmentalizing is rarely helpful. Every issue we face is a kingdom issue worthy of our clear-headed, warm-hearted attention.

Mark's Gospel is filled with examples of righteousness and wickedness and the blessing and judgment that result. For this reason we too must humbly submit to the Teacher. He hasn't stopped teaching. He's still bringing His word which we hear as often as we open the Bible with believing hearts. But the grand message that we learn from Mark's Gospel is that the life that God blesses most is the life of Christ Himself. Mark's story ends with Christ's glory; He is received into heaven to sit at God's right hand. The glory of the gospel is that your life can be so intimately connected with His so as to receive the same benefits that He has earned through His sacrificial service. That is the Christian hope that Mark holds out to us. God says to us today: embrace that hope by believing His good news.

## Questions

1. How can we sanctify the first day of the week, demonstrating that we rejoice in Christ's resurrection?
2. In light of the women's needless concern about the stone covering the grave, how much of your anxiety might be due to fear and not to the realities of life?
3. What does Jesus' reference to Peter in verse 7 tell us about communicating with those who are brought low through sin and repentance?
4. How does Jesus minister to those who demonstrate unbelief and hardness of heart (Mark 16:14)?
5. Reflect on the issue of lethargy in the church today, as well as its cure.
6. How might Mary's meeting with Jesus (v. 9; cf. John 19:11–18) speak to our need to commune with Christ if we hope to succeed in our respective callings?
7. How hard is it to believe when we are overwhelmed by sadness and fear (cf. Mark 16:11)? How can we discipline ourselves to believe even in such a condition?
8. What signs follow them that believe today (cf. Mark 16:17)?

1. Mary Magdalene, who had been healed of demon possession (Luke 8:2), is not to be confused with the sinful woman of Luke 7.

2. Zebedee's wife (Matt. 27:56; Mark 15:40–41). John 19:25 suggests she was Jesus' aunt on his mother's side.

3. It is clear from Matthew (28:2) and Luke (24:4) that the man they saw was one of two angels sent from God to meet these women.

4. William Hendriksen, *Exposition of the Gospel According to Mark*, New Testament Commentary (Grand Rapids: Baker, 1976), 682.

5. The word is used elsewhere at the raising of Jairus's daughter (Mark 5:42), the healing of a paralytic (Luke 5:26), and the healing of a lame man (Acts 3:10; cf. Acts 10:10; 11:5; 22:17).

6. Most textual issues concern a few words or even a single word or spelling.

7. Accessed on May 26, 2015, from http://stillsearching.wordpress.com/2009/03/22/calvinism-so-hot-right-now/.

8. From the "Form for Communion (for those congregations who celebrate the Supper frequently)" in *Acts of Synod London 2010: Seventh Synod of the United Reformed Churches in North America*, 496.

9. As an example, Paul cast out demons and did not die when bitten by a poisonous snake (Acts 28:3–6).

The publisher invites you to respond to us about this book by writing to Reformed Fellowship, Inc., at *president@ reformedfellowship.net*

Founded in 1951, Reformed Fellowship, Inc., is a religious and strictly nonprofit organization composed of a group of Christian believers who hold to the biblical Reformed faith. Our purpose is to advocate and propagate this faith, to nurture those who seek to live in obedience to it, to give sharpened expression to it, to stimulate the doctrinal sensitivities of those who profess it, to promote the spiritual welfare and purity of the Reformed churches, and to encourage Christian action.

Members of Reformed Fellowship express their adherence to the Calvinistic creeds as formulated in the *Belgic Confession*, the *Heidelberg Catechism*, the *Canons of Dort*, and the *Westminster Confession and Catechisms*.

To fulfill our mission, we publish a bimonthly journal, *The Outlook*, and we publish books and Bible study guides. Our website is *www.reformedfellowship.net*